We Would See Jesus

We Would
See Jesus

By George W. Truett

Compiled and edited by
J. B. Cranfill

AMG
PUBLISHERS
Chattanooga, TN 37421

We Would See Jesus

Originally published by
Fleming H. Revell Company

ISBN 0–89957–249–9

Library of Congress Card Catalog Number: 98-87864

Printed in the United States of America
03 02 01 00 99 98 –B– 6 5 4 3 2 1

Contents

Life Sketch of George W. Truett

The life story of George W. Truett had its simple beginning in a quiet farmhouse which nestled in the woods in an escarpment of the Blue Ridge Mountains of North Carolina. His parents were C. L. and Mary Truett. His father, who at the ripe age of eighty–six is still among us, is, himself, a man of mark in his community, and his mother, whom this writer had the pleasure of knowing personally, was one of the most estimable Christian women it has ever been my pleasure to meet.

George W. Truett was reared to farm work, and many were the days that he followed the furrow and harvested the crop on that quiet farm where his father and mother and other loved ones lived and wrought.

Into that home came many important periodicals. While C. L. Truett, the father, was a man of unostentatious life and limited resources, he placed within reach of his children the best literature the world was then producing. Not only that, but also there was a growing library in that home. There were such classics as Bunyan's *Pilgrim's Progress,* Baxter's *Saints' Everlasting Rest,* Pendleton's *Christian Doctrines,* Fox's *Book of Martyrs,* and some choice works of fiction, and upon these the mind of the subject of this sketch fed, grew and expanded with the ongoing of the years.

In his boyhood George W. Truett had limited educational advantages, but such as he had were eagerly grasped, with the result that his mind was enriched and found increasing expansion. At the age of eighteen, he began teaching. A year afterwards he founded the Hiawasse (Georgia) High School, and was its principal for three years. This school drew students from many sections far and near.

It was during his incumbency as principal of this institution that he visited the Georgia Baptist State Convention, an account of which is given in the character sketch appearing in this volume from the pen of Rev. John E. White.

C. L. Truett always had the heart of a pioneer. Many is the time that he looked across the old North Carolina hills and wondered what alluring prospects lay beyond. But it was not until some of his children had found the western trail and landed in Texas that he and his devoted wife moved to Whitewright, Grayson County. Before the parents and other loved ones had made their way to Texas, George W. Truett had dreamed of a college course at Mercer University, but when the entire household had left him, it was not difficult to turn the heart of the young teacher towards the western land. When he was twenty-two years of age, after having established Hiawasse High School upon an enduring foundation, he bade goodbye to the sights and scenes where he had known both trials and triumphs and sped away to Texas.

In 1889 the writer of this sketch resigned the position of financial secretary of Baylor University at Waco to accept, what seemed to him, the larger work of Superintendent of all the Texas Baptist Mission work. Upon his resignation the trustees of Baylor University were much at sea to find one who could successfully take up the work that the former secretary had voluntarily laid down. It was at about this time that a letter came to B. H. Carroll, then and for years before and afterwards president of the Board of Trustees, in which the statement was made that there was a young man at Whitewright, George W. Truett by name, whom the writer believed (and the writer was R. F. Jenkins, one of the best-loved Baptist pastors Texas has ever known) would make an ideal financial secretary for our Waco School.

One sentence in the letter was very impressive. He said, "There is one thing I do know about George W. Truett—wherever he speaks the people do what he asks them to do." The result of this correspondence was that Dr. Carroll asked the young Whitewright preacher to meet him at a missionary mass meeting which was held at McKinney in January, 1891. The result was that George W.

Truett was unanimously elected to this work; he accepted it, moved to Waco, and entered upon the task; and before two years had passed, more than $92,000 (a very large sum then), needed for the emancipation of Baylor University, had been raised, and the school was free. During those trying months the young preacher had the cooperation and help of B. H. Carroll, of whom it can be said there has never been a more loyal, loving, patient, sincere co-laborer and friend.

It was an epochal hour when Baylor was thus freed from debt. The successful financial secretary at once entered Baylor University as a student, and continued his studies there until in 1897 he was graduated with high honors. In the meantime he accepted the call to the pastorate of the East Waco Baptist Church. At that time this fraternity was worshiping in an antiquated, old-time meeting-house which in every way had been long out of date.

George W. Truett has never been able to work under any kind of restraint. He could no more continue to preach in that old house than the eagle could be confined to the cage of the hummingbird. He at once set about the erection of a new, commodious and modern house of worship, with the result that the house was built and dedicated free of debt. During these years he was married to Miss Josephine Jenkins, the much-loved daughter of Judge and Mrs. W. H. Jenkins of Waco.

In the early part of 1897, C. L. Seasholes resigned as pastor of the First Baptist Church at Dallas. This writer was then editor of *The Baptist Standard*. He was asked by Col. W. L. Williams, senior deacon of the First Baptist Church at Dallas, to suggest to him and through him to the church an appropriate man to fill their vacant pastorate. He named George W. Truett. He was quite young—less than thirty years of age. In a large measure he was untried, but the Holy Spirit led this noble fraternity to call him as their pastor. After prayer and deliberation, he came and cast his lot among them. In September of 1897 he officially took charge of the work, which place he has since filled and which pastorate his loving flock hope he will fill to the last day of his earthly life.

His work as pastor and preacher has been a succession of triumphs. Today the First Baptist Church of Dallas is the foremost contributing church in the bounds of the Southern Baptist Convention. It has not only led Texas—but also has led the whole South, and, conditions considered, has led the entire United States, thus verifying that Scripture axiom, "Like people, like priest." With a membership of 2,378, with a Sunday school having an enrollment of between three and four thousand pupils, with aggregate contributions last year of almost $100,000, with conversions and baptisms at practically every service, with a spirit of devotion and service known near and far, this church, under the leadership of their beloved pastor, is pressing on, conquering and to conquer.

Soon after George W. Truett's graduation from Baylor University, its Board of Trustees, with a unanimous and hearty vote, elected him to the presidency of that institution. In this election the alumni, the faculty and the student body heartily joined, and if there was ever pressure brought to bear upon a young man, recently installed in a useful pastorate, to relinquish his charge and enter upon a career of great usefulness in educational leadership, the subject of this sketch felt such pressure. The final battle was fought out by the young pastor on his knees, with the result that his shepherd heart clave to his flock, where it yet abides.

This is not the only call to leave Dallas our friend has had. Calls have come from almost every great city in every state and also from countless organizations and fraternities. If the amount of salary had ever been an object he certainly would have been sorely tempted to leave the western land and plunge into the glare and glamour of some northern or eastern metropolis.

The decision of this pastor to remain with this flock has been amply vindicated. A few years ago, in response to a crying need for more room, the church building was enlarged to practically three times its former seating capacity, and even this early it is found yet to be too small. On some Lord's Day occasions the seating capacity of the new building is severely taxed.

As the years have passed and as the fame of George W. Truett has grown and broadened, the calls upon his time and service have become vastly multiplied. It is not always that he goes to the large and more fruitful fields. Recently he went out to a country place, and there for almost two weeks preached with all the fervor with which he preached when holding a meeting in the city of New York. Many of the country folk were led to Christ and the church and cause were greatly strengthened.

It was an interested and interesting group of his friends and brethren who met together a little more than two years ago to devise a plan for giving their pastor a home. It was promptly provided. It is not in the nature of a parsonage or a pastorium, but was built and given in fee simple to the pastor and his wife. His membership well knew that he would never have a home in any other way. They rejoice that he has this home among them, and it is their cherished hope and wish that he will occupy this home as their pastor until his life's day is done.

The question is constantly arising, "What of this man?" The writer hereof is allowing this answer to be made by another pen, but from his own personal knowledge he essays a modest answer to the query on his own account. The man is one of the most remarkable it has ever been my privilege to know. For liberality of spirit, self-sacrifice, gentleness of heart, purity of character and life, sympathy, helpfulness, liberality and love, this writer does not believe George W. Truett has any superior, and he has few if any peers. He has a heart for all humanity. He is absolutely innocuous to the blandishments of flattery or wealth.

It is no wonder, therefore, that here in Dallas where he has spent a longer period of his life than at any other place except at the home of his boyhood, he is universally beloved. He is called to more houses of mourning, conducts more funerals, consoles more of the bereaved, is the repository of more confidences of the tempest-tossed, the heartbroken and distraught than perhaps any man in this broad land. Not only is he universally beloved in Dallas, where he is best known, but also throughout all Texas his name and self-sacrificing deeds are almost a household word.

He has often given down to his last penny, and then borrowed more money at the bank to give away. He is always hard pressed and will be to the end of his earthly life. The other day the writer of this sketch, when speaking to him, told him of a gift a mutual friend had made to a bereaved home in order to help defray the funeral expenses. The pastor, with those searching eyes turned upon the writer, said: "That is what money is for, and that is all it is for."

His work seems but just begun. He is now in the flood-tide of his greatest usefulness and power. He has not yet reached the half-century mark, and it is not too much to hope that before his earthly days shall end he will achieve new heights of usefulness of which now we scarcely dare to dream.

J. B. CRANFILL
Dallas, Texas 1915

George W. Truett, the Man and Preacher

The following character sketch was written some years since when Dr. Truett held a meeting with Dr. White, who was then pastor of the Second Baptist Church, Atlanta, GA.

In the gallery of the South's strong men—men who are at the front of moral leadership in her marvelous progress—the picture of George W. Truett would not lack much of the foremost place were the vote left to the admiration of the more than two million white Baptists of the Southern Baptist Convention.

The coming of this Texanic-Carolina-Georgian to preach in the Second Baptist Church, Atlanta, during the Concerted Baptist Evangelistic Campaign is therefore an event of more than ordinary interest.

Call him "Texanic," because he comes from Texas and brings the Texan breadth and sweep atmospherically with him; Texanic being something better than titanic, more pervasive, more comprehensive of a certain great quality that encircles men who come within George Truett's area.

Call him "Carolina," because he sprang out of the rough, mountainous territory of the Old North State, drew his breath from its hills, received its birthmark on his spirit. It is a rude, rough country, but its crops are men. Think of hardest, most stubborn land, the simplest, most backward section of modern American life—untouched by railroads, not a half-dozen comfortable churches, less than seventy days' annual free school term, supported out of less than one dollar per capita free school funds and yet the land of red blood and new brain cells, and you have Clay County, North Carolina, as George Truett knew it in his youth.

He was born near the county seat, Hayesville, in the year 1867.

Call him also "Georgian," because Georgia gave him his growing pains—perhaps his initial thrust forward. It was in 1889, in the courthouse at Marietta, Georgia, that his star first scintillated strikingly. The scene is worthy a picture in the Baptist Valhalla.

The Georgia Baptist Convention was in session. Ferd C. McConnell, not yet himself known to fame as "Forensic Cyclone McConnell," the present distinguished leader of Atlanta, Georgia, was down from the mountains of Rabun County with the story of the struggle for the mountain boys and girls at Hiawasse.

"They are there," he shouted, "like gold for the touch of the miner's pick and they are fit to stand in the presence of kings, packed full of brains and character waiting for a chance. If you don't believe it I'll show you! George! Where is George Truett?" George not being forthcoming immediately the orator called again, "Brethren, I do believe he's got skeered and run off." Then someone in the rear of the courthouse said, "Here he is." A pale, twenty-two-year-old mountain youth was forced out in the aisle and obediently up to the prisoners' dock, looking half-frightened and vastly embarrassed by the focus of eyes. "Brethren, this is George Truett and he can speak like Spurgeon. George, tell them what the Lord has done for you and what you are trying to do up in the mountains."

Then George began. It was a simple story, but epic in its pathos of quiet recital of the hopes and passions of an unsung heroism.

It was a story of struggle for the lives of others who might have what had been denied to him—a college education. It grew larger with each word—till every heart was thrilling with that plaintive, pleading sort of voice which carries so well the burden of tears which seem ever laid on it. But the speech was no pitiful plea of poverty—who ever heard that out of a Southern mountaineer? It was rather the cry of the youth who bore the banner with the strange device—Excelsior, the strong persuasion of a just matter, the logic of one who, denied himself, was resolved to let his lack plead for others.

Dr. J. B. Hawthorne, then at the crowning of his great career in Atlanta, was one of those who sat heartbroken under the mastery of that speech. This was his testimony:

"I have heard Henry Grady at his highest, but never in my life has my soul been so swept as that boy from the mountains swept it that day in the courthouse in Marietta."

Another great Georgian was present on that occasion—Calder B. Willingham, of Macon. He at once arose and said, "I want the honor of giving that young man a college education. If he will come to Macon I will pay his expenses at Mercer University, till he graduates." Then and there the compact was sealed, the convention being witness. The youth went back to the mountains with something to say to his old friends—the peaks of Rabun and the clouds and the God he knew face to face behind great nature's thin veil, of a new hope and a great joy set before him.

Strange is Providence! The pat of George Truett's life did not lie towards Macon. He never saw Mercer University, and yet I think till this day he regards himself as a sort of alumnus of Mercer University, as one of those shadowy sons who dreamed their course through her halls.

With September 1889, no boy, but a letter, went to Mr. Willingham. His father had resolved upon Texas. A man in years, but a son in loyalty, went with that resolve out of the mountains of North Georgia to the great new land as blindly in sheer obedience, and I doubt not as faithfully as Abraham went into Canaan. Now, what will the prophets say of this? Listen: That boy will go to Texas; in less than four years he will save a college from financial despair and endow it; in four years more he will graduate from it, and in five years more he will be elected to its presidency. Well, that is what George W. Truett did in Texas.

But he is not the president of Baylor University. This is a very interesting fact to us just now in Atlanta. He is a preacher. Dear old billboarded, newspapered, sensation-surfeited Atlanta; agog yesterday over Elbert Hubbard and today over Fluffy Raffles, but she has one saving clause: She loves a preacher if he is a real preacher. George Truett will win Atlanta wholesomely. He will win here as he wins in the West by being what he is, a man who means it without trying to. What he is speaks as loudly as what he says. He is a preacher. That is the point of his distinction. He is content to be that. He is an evangel, not evangelist. There is not an "ist" nor a twist in all his make-up. Plain, mountain-hearted, love-torn George Truett, the man who woos cowboys in Texas to their knees, wins cities also.

People will come from hearing him preach in the Second Baptist Church asking themselves what it is that constitutes the acknowledged power of his preaching. And they will get various answers, but in one all opinion will meet. It is something in the man himself—the man behind the sermon, and in it through and through as an incarnation of truthfulness in a messenger. Many sermons will bear understanding and yield to analysis their secret of charm as sermons. I doubt if the newspapers were ever meant for George Truett, though many of his sermons have been reported in full. He belongs preeminently to that class of preachers who illustrate the claim that the press can never usurp the function of the pulpit; who convince us that preaching is in the highest sense an incarnation, something more than a report of the truth, something more than the proclamation of the gospel.

George Whitfield could so speak the most commonplace words as to send chills through his audience. George Truett has much of this power to communicate to men his soul on the most ordinary vehicles of thought and language. His adjectives and adverbs take on its spiritual quality as the dull black wire takes on the electric current.

Electricity, however, is scarcely a fortunate figure. He is least of all of the spectacular type. There is nothing angular or irregular in him. He has none of the personality run to seed—individualism on a pious spree. The strongest personalities are not eccentric. Eccentricity is unnecessary to such men. They have specific gravity beyond the need of peculiar advertisement. Too much of what men call personality in the pulpit, in the view that preaching is an incarnation, must hinder rather than help the gospel purpose. Is it possible that evangelism, which, reduced to the terms of psychology, is egotism, can be the appointed power of God unto salvation? At least George

W. Truett's power, as a preacher, can have no such explanation. "Heart power" is the phrase most often employed to explain him. Ask somebody what they mean by that. It is not as easy as it seems.

With George Truett before my mind's eye—"heart power" is just what seems to me the only vital power of the gospel of Jesus Christ.

Translated into the visible, audible, realizable fact soon to stand in the pulpit of the Second Baptist Church, "heart power" is this:

A man of substantial flesh, enough to be a man of like passions with other men; an open Saxon face—a serious face, some say a sad face.

A voice set to a very pronounced key of pathos—a cadence that individualizes his speech. Alas, for those who attempt to pilfer it! An impression of unfeigned sympathy, as of a man who has suffered, and whose pain, whatever it be, has become lost in a larger pain, through exchange of all personal life sorrows for the great human sorrow everywhere.

In declining the presidency of Baylor University he said simply in explanation: "I have sought and found the shepherd's heart." Perhaps this is the real secret of George W. Truett's unique place in Texas and among the Southern Baptists.

Many lips have quoted the great avowal which F. W. D. Meyer puts into the mouth of Paul the apostle, but none whom I know can appropriate it more seriously than George W. Truett, when he stands up before a congregation of his fellow men to preach the gospel that saves.

> Oft when the word is on me to deliver,
>   Lifts the illusion and the truth lies bare,
> Desert or throng, the city or the river
>   Melts in a lucid paradise of air.
>
> Only like souls I see the folk thereunder
>   Bound who should conquer, slaves who
>   should be kings;
> Hearing their one hope with an empty wonder,
>   Sadly contented in a show of things.

Then with a rush the intolerable craving
  Shivers throughout me like a trumpet call.
Oh, to save these, to perish for their saving,
  Die for their life, He offered for them all.

Rev. John E. White

1
We Would See Jesus

We would see Jesus (John 12:21).

The age-long cry of the human race has been for the revelation of a personal God, able and willing to forgive human sin, and to give rest to the human conscience. From the days of Job, man's cry has been "Oh, that I knew where I might find Him!" Plato voiced such cry when he said, "We look for a God, or a God-inspired man, who will show us our duty and take away the darkness of our eyes." Through long generations of Jewish history there thrilled the longing, and was voiced the prophetic hope of a coming Messiah, able and willing to meet man's deepest needs. In the fullness of time He came, and the fame of His words and deeds soon filled the land. A great feast was had in Jerusalem, and along with the thousands who attended it there came some Greeks, whose cry also was "We would see Jesus." That was the first voice from the outside world that gave a hint of the awakening of its sleeping conscience to the fact that Jesus was to be the Savior and Sovereign over the Gentile as well as the Jewish world.

Marvelous was the impression made upon Jesus by that outside cry. It came at an hour when His work seemed ready to fail; but from that hour there was a new tone of triumph in His words. No more do we hear His plaintive cry over unbelieving Jerusalem; but His thoughts are bravely turned towards Calvary, and His victorious shout is "The hour is come that the Son of Man should be glorified. Verily, verily, I say unto you, except a corn of wheat fall into the ground and die, it abideth alone; but if it die, it bringeth forth much fruit." He speaks again: "Now is my soul troubled; and what shall I say? Father, save Me from this hour: but for this cause came I unto this hour. Father, glorify Thy name. Then came there a voice from heaven, saying, 'I have glorified it and will glorify it again.'" His heart thrills with the sense of His glorious mission, and He speaks again: "Now is the judgment of this world; now shall the prince of this world be cast out. And I, if I be lifted up from the earth, will draw all men unto Me."

Why would we see Jesus? We may well wish to see Him, because of what He was and is in His own personality. He was both God and man, the God-Man, in one person. Never did hyphen elsewhere mean so much as here, the God-Man. It both joins and divides. It marks distinction and yet unity. Jesus was as really God as though He were never man, and as really man as though He were never God. In the face of this truth, well might the chief apostle say, "Without controversy, great is the mystery of godliness: God was manifest in the flesh, justified in the Spirit, seen of angels, preached unto the Gentiles, believed on in the world, received up into glory." The most stupendous truth ever submitted to human thought is that stated in John's five simple words: "The Word was made flesh."

In the study of Jesus we need always to begin with His humanity. That is where the early disciples began, and that is the rational order. A proper conception of His humanity must be the basis for a proper understanding of His divine nature and work.

In these days men sometimes tell us of their difficulties concerning the deity of Jesus, rather than His humanity. In the earlier days, unbelief made its stoutest assaults upon His humanity. The earlier heresies were gnostic heresies that denied that Jesus was really a man. One school of gnostics held that the body of Jesus did not belong essentially to His nature, but that the Messiah descended upon Jesus at His baptism, and left Him before His death. Another school held that His body was but a mere illusion, a veneer of human nature, with Godhood hidden behind the face of a man. And still another school held that His body was a body from heaven, having nothing in common with earth.

Against all such theories the title which Jesus chose for Himself attests His true and real humanity. "He took not on Him the form of angels; but He took on Him the seed of Abraham." He was a vital part of the race that He came to save, bone of its bone and flesh of its flesh. He had a human mother and a human birth. He grew, as did others, in wisdom and in stature. His feelings and needs were as those of other men. He was weary and hungry and thirsty. He craved human companionship and sympathy. He was "a man of sorrows and acquainted with grief." "Wherefore, in all things, it behooved Him to be made like unto His brethren, that He might be a merciful and faithful High Priest, in all things pertaining to God to make reconciliation for the sins of the people."

Behold Him, not "A Son of Man," but "The Son of Man," for all humanity was summed up in Him. He was the one perfect, ideal, complete man. "Which of you convinceth Me of sin?" was and is His fearless challenge. "I find no fault in Him" was and is the universal testimony of His friends and foes. In Himself Jesus combines all those gracious qualities that abode severally in His people. If we would look for the highest example of meekness, we would not look to Moses, but to Jesus, who was unapproachably meek and lowly in heart. For the highest example of patience we would not look to Job, but to Jesus, who, when He was reviled, reviled not again. For the highest example of wisdom we would not look to Solomon, but to Jesus, who spake as never man spake. For the highest example of consuming pity we would not look to weeping Jeremiah, but to Jesus, as alone He weeps over Jerusalem. For the highest example of soul-absorbing zeal we would not look to Paul, but to Jesus, of whom it was said: "The zeal of thine house hath eaten me up." For the highest example of love we would not look to John, but to Jesus, who, while we were His enemies, loved us and gave Himself for us. All other men have but fragmentary goodness and greatness; that of Jesus is complete, perfect, wanting nothing. The searchlight of criticism has been focused on Jesus through the long centuries, and yet it has failed to find in Him one suggestion of sin, one ill-spoken word, one selfish deed. Men talk about not believing in miracles. What will they do with Jesus of Nazareth? He is the preeminent miracle of all the ages. Who was that one and only perfect man? Was He not more than a man?

The only rational solution of the humanity of Jesus is the acknowledgment of His deity. For men to laud Jesus as a great and good man, while they repudiate His deity, is to involve themselves in logical contradictions and moral inconsistencies which it is impossible either to reconcile or understand. Remember the claims that this wise and holy One makes for Himself: "I am the light of the world." "No man cometh unto the Father but by Me." "He that hath seen Me hath seen the Father." "I and the Father are one." "Come unto Me, all ye that labor and are heavy laden and I will give you rest." If Jesus Christ be not more than a man, what must be thought of the presumption and vanity of these mighty claims? How is it that man's conscience accepts without protest or hesitancy these mighty claims? That question must forever remain an insoluble mystery on any other premise than that Jesus was God manifest in the flesh, in whom dwells all the fullness of the Godhead bodily. From His cradle to His grave the proofs of His Godhead were, in His own person, finding constant illustration. The shepherds came to salute Him as king, and the magi, with their rich gifts, came from the Far East to worship Him, while He was yet a tiny babe upon His mother's heart. While a lad only twelve years of age, His superlative wisdom utterly astounded the learned doctors in the temple. As a young man he patiently wrought at the workman's bench, teaching us how the Infinite One can calmly wait, girt with the consciousness of His divine mission. When He came to prosecute His public ministry, He had only to speak the word and the winds were hushed, the storms calmed, the hungry thousands fed, the sick made well and the dead brought back to life. He lived as none other ever lived. He died as none other ever died, and from Olivet He went back to His Father the consummator of history, the victorious Savior of a lost world.

"We would see Jesus," not only because of what He is in His matchless person, but, also, because of what He is and does for man. He is man's Savior from sin. "Thou shalt call His name Jesus, for He shall save His people from their sins." If Jesus were merely a perfect example or a matchless teacher for man, then He could not encompass man's deepest needs. Sin is the terrible tragedy, the intolerable yoke in every human life. Our highest and eternal joy in seeing Jesus is in seeing Him as our Savior from sin. By His expiatory death on the cross, "the just for the unjust," Jesus answers the eternally vital question how a guilty sinner may have forgiveness and salvation and happiness here and forevermore.

> Forever God, forever man,
> My Jesus shall endure:
> And fixed on Him my hope remains
> Eternally secure.

It was said of Mozart that he brought angels down, and of Beethoven that he lifted mortals up. Jesus does both and more. He is God's way to man, He is man's way to God, the true Jacob's ladder between earth and heaven.

And the glorious truth is that His gospel may be put into the crucible of human experience. Man may personally know whether Jesus can give peace to the troubled conscience, whether He can give light for life's bedarkened problems, whether He can give healing for earth's staggering sorrows. The world is filled with men and women, this hour, who have vainly sought everywhere for peace and light and help, but they found it not until they found it in Jesus. These men and women have tested Him, and in their deepest consciousness they know better than they know anything else that through Him their darkness has been dispelled, their burdens lifted, their victories won. Tell me how it is that, of all the sons of men since the world began, it was never heard that a man was saved by Plato, or by Socrates, or by any one else but by Jesus Christ alone. How is it that He alone has been able really to redeem men from the fatal grip of appetite and passion and sin? There can be but one logically intelligent answer, and that answer is, that in Jesus

Christ we have the only begotten Son of God, God of God, Light of Light, very God of very God, the one divine and all-sufficient Savior.

How may we see Jesus? May we see Jesus today? Not, to be sure, with our physical eyes, but with the eyes of the mind and heart. May we approach Him, realize Him, be conscious of His personal presence and help, even as we are conscious of the presence and help of parent, or teacher, or dearest earthly friend? These are vital questions that go to the depths of our hearts. I make bold to answer them that Jesus may be, ought to be, more real to us than is any other person in all the world. Jesus is not some mere theory, some inspiring memory, some vague, personal influence; but He is a Person, to be approached, to be felt, to be trusted, to be loved, and to be obeyed even unto death. How may we thus see Jesus as we are daily driven by the manifold problems and duties of the earthly life?

If we would see Jesus, we must make much of His Book. If we would know a person, we must understand him. If we would trust a person, then our trust must be based on knowledge. Jesus cannot be seen, will not be graciously real to the man who neglects the Bible. It is true that "the heavens declare the glory of God, and the firmament showeth His handiwork." But, left to nature, the Bible taken away, man cannot know how to love and trust and obey Him properly. Though man might name every star that blazes in the eternal depths; though he might map the heavens and tell the constellations as his familiar friends; though he might understand the voice of the flowers; though he might catch the monologues of the mountains, the dirges of the oceans, the symphonies of the spheres; though all nature might speak to him the mighty secrets of its origin and Maker, in all this man would see only the majesty and mightiness of God. In God's hand would be the sword of justice, on His lips the word of wisdom, and around Him the resplendent robe of righteousness, at once man's envy and despair. Only in the Bible may man find out the mercy of God, in the forgiveness of sins, through Jesus Christ.

Other books may be read, some of them with much profit; God's book must be read, and read humbly, reverently, earnestly,

continuously, if we would see much of Jesus. If you have read the
life of Chinese Gordon, one of the noblest Christians of his or any
other age, you discerned that the secret of that wonderful life was
in the fact that he spent long hours every day in the study of the
Bible. He had many books in the Soudan, but this was the testimony that he left concerning them: "I may as well part with all my
books except two, the Bible and the Concordance, so far as they
contain essential knowledge."

If we would see Jesus, we must know much of secret prayer—
mark you, of secret prayer. Secret prayer is the unerring ther-
mometer to our life of prayer. If ever we are sincere in prayer, it is
when we are in secret prayer. It is then, if ever, that we are conscious
of God. Jesus said, "But thou, when thou prayest, enter into thy
closet, and when thou hast shut thy door, pray to thy Father
which is in secret; and thy Father which seeth in secret shall reward
thee openly." How much do we give ourselves to secret prayer? Is
it not just here that most of all we fail? We go about the doing of
many things, but is not secret prayer one of the things that we
largely leave undone? It takes time to become spiritual, and time
spent alone with God is the best spent time in all one's life.

Again, if we would see Jesus, we must watch against sin, with
uncompromising warfare. There must be absolute sincerity and
wholehearted thoroughness at this point. That were but hollow
mockery for a man to pray for forgiveness, his own heart the while
burning with hatred and festering with grudges against some fellow creature. The amputating knife of genuine repentance must be
put to sin, if we would hope for the smile of Jesus and for the benefit of His blood which cleanseth from all sin. God can't afford to
answer some men's prayers! For Him to do so would be to put a
premium upon sin. The hidden wedge of gold and the Babylonish
garment must be disclosed and restored, if men may hope for answered prayer. It is sin that separates between man and God. It is
sin that cuts the nerve of all acceptable prayer. Sin is a veil through
which Jesus cannot be seen. Sin is an insulator that turns away the
currents between man and God. It is "the supplication of a righteous man that availeth much." "If I regard iniquity in my heart, the

Lord will not hear me." No man who is not keenly sensitive to sin can know much or see much of Jesus. "Blessed are the pure in heart, for they shall see God"—see Him here and now in daily experience. "Who shall ascend into the hill of the Lord? Or who shall stand in His holy place? He that hath clean hands and a pure heart, who hath not lifted up his soul unto vanity nor sworn deceitfully. He shall receive the blessing of the Lord, and righteousness from the God of his salvation." Oh, what need have we for frequent and most rigid self-examination, that we may become increasingly sensitive to every approach of sin. And we are to watch with all diligence against the little sins. It was the little foxes that spoiled the vines. If we carelessly cherish what may seem to us to be inconsequential sins, for example, pride, which goeth before destruction, and envy, which is as rottenness in the bones, these sins will consume us as doth a cancer and more and more will they hide from us the face of Jesus.

If we would see Jesus, we need to magnify the blessedness of Christian fellowship. The old-fashioned experience-meeting, when men and women came together just to tell, timidly though joyfully, what they saw and felt and knew of the things of Jesus—would to God our churches had it back again! "Then they that feared the Lord spake often one to another, and the Lord hearkened and heard it, and a book of remembrance was written before Him for them that feared the Lord, and that thought on His name." Sometimes a preacher's sermonic fires burn low, and not a text will give up its treasures, dig for them though he may. What does the preacher do? Let such preacher find and talk with someone who has a vital knowledge of the saving grace of God, and sermonic fires will immediately burn again.

Once again, if we would see Jesus, we must be busy for Him. The indolent Christian cannot see much or know much of Jesus. Idleness is one of the most terrible foes to grace. It is the running stream that is the healthy stream. The stagnant pond breeds miasma and malaria and death. Many a Christian who is spiritually sick, he knows not why, would thrill with a new joy and new visions of Jesus if only he would be busy for Him. Doubt, unbelief, despondency are all cut to pieces by activity. It is the man who does Christ's will unto whom is revealed His doctrine.

And still again, if we would see Jesus as we ought and as we may, we must give ourselves completely to His guidance and government. Jesus will be Lord of all, or He will not be Lord at all. The reason why so many people get so little out of their religion is that they put so little into it. If men would see Jesus, see Him to the deepest joy of their hearts, and from Him have the noblest victories in their lives, then, for all this, they must pay the requisite price. Paul paid such price. Gladly did he suffer the loss of all things, home, kindred, inheritance, comforts, country, life itself, that he might have the excellency of the knowledge of Christ Jesus, his Lord. Do you wonder that he had visions and revelations which could not be put into speech? Do you wonder that his letters abound in doxologies, as he contemplates the unfolding glory of his Lord? Paul paid the price for his glorious visions of Jesus.

Here, then, is the vital question for us. Will we pay the price to see Jesus as we need to see Him, as He would have us see Him? Are we willing to live for Him, to put Him first, to do His will, be what it may, lead where it will? Right here is the supreme battle of the Christian life. It is the battle between Christ and self. The self-centered life will not see Jesus, and must surely fail. The Christ-centered life will mount higher and higher in its visions of Jesus, and will more and more exult in the victory that overcomes the world. George MacDonald well puts this truth in simple verse:

> I said, "Let me walk in the fields";
>   He said, "Nay, walk in the town";
> I said, "There are no flowers there";
>   He said, "No flowers, but a crown."
> I said, "But the sky is black,
>   There is nothing but noise and din";
> But He wept as He sent me back—
>   "There is more," He said, "there is sin."
> I said, "But the air is thick
>   And fogs are veiling the sun";

He answered, "Yet souls are sick,
  And souls in the dark undone."

I said, "I shall miss the light,
  And friends will miss me, they say";

He answered me, "Choose tonight
  If I am to miss you, or they."

I pleaded for time to be given;
  He said, "Is it hard to decide?

It will not seem hard in heaven
  To have followed the steps of your Guide."

I cast one look at the fields,
  Then set my face to the town;

He said: "My child, do you yield?
  Will you leave the flowers for the crown?"

Then into His hand went mine,
  And into my heart came He,

And I walk in a light divine,
  The path I had feared to see.

Oh, men and women, if we will pay the price, we may daily see
Jesus—may know that He walks with us, talks with us, and lives
with us, and lives in us, our certain help for every day and duty of
earth. And thus seeing Him and serving Him, brighter and better
shall be all our days, even unto that blissful day when we shall pass
through the gates of the celestial city, where we shall be "like Him,
for we shall see Him as He is."

2
A Prayer for a Revival

Wilt Thou not revive us again: that Thy people may rejoice in Thee? (Ps. 85:6).

The text is a short prayer, but volumes of meaning are wrapped up in it. God give us tonight to pray it from the very depths of our hearts! It is a prayer for God's people. "Will Thou not revive us again: that Thy people may rejoice in Thee?" David does not pray about conditions or circumstances, that these may be changed, but he prays for people, for God's people. "Wilt Thou not revive us again, that Thy people may rejoice in Thee?" For David had learned the lesson far back in that olden time, that if there be any deep, great work of grace wrought for the world that is lost, then such work of grace will begin in the hearts of God's people. It is true and does not need to be argued that, when God's people are right, things always go well with His work; and when God's people are wrong, things go badly with His work.

It is a lesson that comes down to us through all the generations, that, going before any great, deep work of grace, God's people have waited before Him in confession of sin, in supplication for His grace, in the humbling of their hearts, in the submission of their

11

wills to Him, that He might do for them and with them according to His holy will. That is surely the lesson that comes down to
us, touching God's work and people all through the generations.
There is no such thing, brethren, as any great, deep, far-reaching
work of grace anywhere, if God's people do not experimentally
know the mighty means of prayer touching such work of grace. All
history as it touches God's people and His work in the world is the
confirmation of this statement. When Israel down in Egypt prayed
after the right fashion, then it was that deliverance came. In the days
of Nehemiah, when God's work had run down, and when Nehemiah, with the faithful ones about him, waited upon God for its
reviving and its rebuilding, when they prayed after the right fashion, the walls of God's house went up again. It was so in the days
of good King Josiah. The thing that preeminently characterized the
revival for the glory of God in his time was the right waiting before God of His people. And surely the one marvelous thing about
that incomparable meeting on the Day of Pentecost, the influence
of which kept on in such wondrous fashion for a generation;
surely the one marvelous thing about that meeting, from the
human view-point, was, that for ten days God's people just prayed.
For ten long days they tarried yonder in the quiet place, away from
the crowd, waiting, with one accord, for power from on high. When
will we learn the lesson, brethren, that it is time gained in all respects
if we give ourselves very, very much to the blessed exercise of prayer
in carrying on God's work in the world? For my part, I do not believe that in any of these "revival" or "special meetings" that we have
that God is honored in them, or that people are really regenerated
in them, if going through them and before them and after them
there is not the moving of the hearts of God's people in prayer.

When will we rightly lay such great matter to heart? It is fundamental to the real success of all God-saving effort. And you
yourselves are the witnesses that I speak the truth tonight. In your
own Christian experiences, out from the past, even as I talk, there
come to you the memories of the occasions when you were specially blessed of God in the winning of souls. Those mighty spiritual blessings that came to you; those days of the right hand of God;

those days when you heard His stately steppings; those days when you saw His mighty Spirit pierce the hearts of sinful men and bring them down, those were the times when your own hearts were empty of their self-sufficiency, and when with a cry unto God from the deepest depths of the soul, you besought Him to arise and plead His own cause, and save lost sinners for whom Christ died. You yourselves, I say, are witnesses to that same significant truth. When you have had special power with men to win them to God, it was always when you had power with God. And men do not have power with God—it is a thing unknown in His spiritual kingdom—if they be not men of prayer, men of real intercession, men who know the meaning of the secret place, where alone they look into the King's face until He speaks His message to them. There is no such thing as power to win lost men to God if His people do not pray. You yourselves, I say, are witnesses to that great fact. The times when you have had power with men so that they could not resist your appeals, so that you saw their faces humbled before you, and you saw the conquest of the soul go on before your very eyes, those were the times when you were in touch with the great King, when your soul had conscious fellowship with Him, when you took hold of Him and felt that you were one with Him. Men who come to realize that experience do so through the gracious medium of prayer.

"The burden of the Lord," when that is upon them, then it is that men know the burden of prayer. O brethren, this light, easy, tearless, hop, skip and jump method in the matchless work of turning men to God is not the New Testament way. If men are turned to Almighty God in any blessed fashion, then the people of God know about it, and there is a cry unto Him, the deepest cry of their hearts is heard, that lost sinners may be saved. God's people always cry like that if any mighty movement of His Spirit and His saving grace is felt among the people.

"The burden of the Lord," when that is upon them, then it is that men know the burden of prayer. O brethren, this light, easy, tearless, hop, skip and jump method in the matchless work of turning men to God is not the New Testament way. If men are turned to Almighty God in any blessed fashion, then the people of God know about it, and there is a cry unto Him, the deepest cry of their hearts is heard, that lost sinners may be saved. God's people always cry like that if any mighty movement of His Spirit and His saving grace is felt among the people.

When I was a little lad, I recall how that again and again I went to the old country church to their appointed "protracted meetings" every summer; and the farmers would gather in at the morning meetings, and then again at the evening meetings, two services a day, and they would thus daily gather together for several days. Great crowds came, but often nothing seemed to be done. I have seen and heard those farmers, as they would meet and chat under the great trees before the morning service. Often they would talk about this and that and then one would say to the other, "Neighbor, have you any burden for souls today?" and the answer would come back rather shrinkingly, "No, neighbor, I haven't any special burden, yet, for souls, I am sorry to say." And the next day that would be repeated. They would thus talk around on the edges of the meeting, maybe for days, and then one would say: "Have you any burden about this meeting today? Have you any burden for souls today?" And the answer would be with trembling lip and with eyes suffused with tears: "I have, O neighbor, I have. God is my judge, how last night I felt to call upon Him through the long, long night, and I saw my own boys lost, and I saw your boys lost, and I saw our neighborhood lost. Oh, I have a burden for souls I cannot describe." I was at first too small to know what it all meant, but I can recall with what awe I would listen to it all, and even as a little child my soul was perfectly sure that God was somewhere near. And He was! And when we would go into the old country meeting house, on such a day, and the meeting would begin, and trembling lips would lead the prayers, and the hymns would be sung, God would come down into that meeting, and men that day were brought down by the life-giving Spirit of God. Whereas for days before, the meetings were perfunctory and stilted and cold, now they were kindled into a strange glow. Sobs were heard on every side, and lost men asked, "What must we do to be saved?" What had happened, brethren? That "burden of souls" had come to God's people, with-out which soul-winning effort is largely in vain. Whenever they have that "burden of souls," things glorious always come to pass in the kingdom of God.

We had better wait; we had better betake ourselves to the quiet place; we had better search our hearts, and beg Him to search them for us; we had better go alone, each one for himself or herself, and talk with God, each one pouring out his soul to this effect: "O God, give me to feel about Thy work like Thou wishest. Come down in Thine own way, and open the gates to my soul, so that I shall feel about Thy work as Thou wishest." You and I need to do that, brethren, and we need to do that tonight, with special reference to the work that is just now before us.

Some months ago a pastor was out in a vast country camp-meeting. A large arbor was provided, and from night to night there gathered a mighty crowd, so that the pastor needed to put his voice out to the last limit to be heard. But for days, so far as could be judged, nothing much was done. One night the preacher went to his room, and was making ready to retire, when the gentleman with whom he stopped came in. The host had very little to say, and the preacher made ready for sleep, and now was in the bed, while the host sat there on the cot on the other side of the room. Both slept in the same room. The good wife of the host was gone, having departed a few years before, to be with the Lord. He had two grown daughters, popular and beautiful, but worldly—worldly, it seemed, after an unusual fashion. He sat over there that night on his cot, and after a while, just as the preacher was ready to sleep, a sob was heard, and the preacher looked up, and beheld his kindly friend with his face in his hands, and his great body fairly quiver-ing. Said the preacher, "What is the trouble?" calling his host by name. He answered, "You ought to know what the trouble is. You have been in my home for three or four days. You ought to know what the trouble is." The preacher said, "Yes, I do; it is the girls." The host replied, "It is even so. Their mother is gone, and the sense of responsibility for them comes over me tonight as I never felt it be-fore in all my life." Then he added, "Oh, if Mary (that was the older

one) would only come to Christ, if she would only come to
Christ, the problem, I think, would be settled with Jennie. Jennie
always does what Mary does." The preacher said, "Well, we will pray
for Mary tonight," and out of his bed he came, and knelt by his host.
They talked to God about Mary, specifically about her, that the
Almighty Savior might Himself take hold of her heart, and bring
her to Himself. She was an amiable, beautiful girl, as has been said,
but utterly indifferent about the claims of the soul, so far as could
be seen. Then the preacher went back to his bed. After a while the
door stood ajar, and the anxious father was seen quietly going out
through the moonlight, and then the door was closed, and the
preacher was soon asleep. In the early morning time the door was
again quietly opened, and in came the host. A glance at his cot
showed that he had been absent for the night. The preacher asked,
"Where have you been?" And the answer was "I will tell you
about it, but you need not speak of it to the others. It is not a matter to be spoken of. I have been out there all night long talking to
God about Mary; and that is not all. Mary will come to Christ
today." Said the preacher, "Do you look for that?" He simply answered, "Yes, you will see that blessed result today." And that day,
when the preacher finished his sermon at the morning meeting, and
asked, while they sang, if anybody had found the Savior, to come
and confess Him before all the people, before they could start the
music at all, Mary came, with smiling face, and said, "I found Him
while you preached." Do you doubt, my brethren, that there was a
vital connection between that man's prayer and that child's return
to Christ? The very next day, before the preacher had preached ten
minutes, the other daughter, Jennie, rose up in the midst of the great
crowd, and said, "Papa, I have found the Savior, too." I ask again, do
you doubt that there was a vital connection between that prayer and
that child's return to Christ? O God, burden us for souls! Burden
us for souls! Ah, Paul had the "burden for souls." Hear him: "I say
the truth in Christ, I lie not, my conscience also bearing me witness in the Holy Ghost, that I have great heaviness and continual
sorrow in my heart. For I could wish that myself were accursed
from Christ, for my brethren, my kinsmen, according to the flesh."

The "burden for souls"—may God give it to us all! This is God's way—may His way be ours!

Why is this God's way? The reasons for it could be multiplied. Here are some. This is God's plan. Because in His own infinite wisdom He chose that it should be His plan, that is enough for us. God has revealed all along that one of the mightiest instruments in His kingdom for the furtherance of His cause in this world, for the turning of men to Christ, is prayer. See the injunctions to us to pray. We are to pray without ceasing. We are to pray for all men. We are not to so sin against the Lord, and so sin against men, as to cease praying for men. Behold how the Scriptures magnify the place of prayer in the kingdom of God for the furtherance of His truth. It is God's plan, and we are to address ourselves to God's plan. Whenever we know God's mind about anything, then we have reached the end of the debate. We are to obey Him unreservedly.

And, then, we go further, and see that as labor is good for us in the world physical, so is it in the world spiritual. Spiritual labor is an exercise of incalculable moment. As in the physical world physical labor is for our upbuilding; in the world spiritual, spiritual labor, the exercising of ourselves unto Godliness, is the thing made very much of in the Scriptures.

Nor is that all. This kind of waiting upon God, this kind of confession of helplessness, and of supplication for grace and power, fits us to take care of people when they are saved. O brethren, how sad it is that our young Christians, so many times, get such a pitiful start in the Christian life! It is a great thing for a Christian to be well born, and that is one reason why we need to guard the churches of Jesus Christ. The churches of Jesus Christ are the supreme centers of evangelization. One of the things we have most earnestly to protest against, in these times, is the carrying away of evangelistic efforts from the churches of Jesus Christ. The churches are the hotbeds wherein the plants are to be grown to the Savior's honor. This is certainly a time when the churches need to give their most vigorous and faithful attention to this meaningful truth. Ring it out everywhere that the churches are the centers where evangelistic effort may be most wisely conducted. When Christ's church is spiritual, and calls upon Him with all humility, and with self-abnegation, and He answers back, and gives them a soul saved, then the church is ready to take care of that soul. Why is that in very many of our churches vast numbers remain little spiritual babes all their lives? The answer is their start was bad. Their surroundings were not of a gracious sort. They were not put on the right track, and kept going on the right track. We are ready to take care of the young converts, when they come to us, in answer to the right sort of prayer. What would become of that little newborn babe if it should be taken from its mother's arms, and thrown into the snow-banks? And what will become of the little newborn child of God if it be ushered into a church where the atmosphere is lukewarm, and worldly, and indifferent to God's claims? There is likely to be one outcome, only, to that little religious life. The shipwreck of happiness and usefulness, for the most part. Our God has ordained this great method of carrying on His work, so that when souls are given to us, we are able to take care of them after the right fashion.

Not only that, but this is His plan, in order to teach us what we seem to forget most quickly of all—salvation is of the Lord. That is the truth that we seem to learn last of all, and the truth that we seem to forget most quickly of all—salvation is of the Lord. Oh, we accept it theoretically. You ask if we believe it, and with great promptness we answer that we do, and yet, do we? How much do we believe it? How long we are forgetting that vital truth, that we can raise men from that cemetery yonder as easily as we can regenerate the most amiable child in your Sunday school to God—that we can speak a world like this into life as easily as we can regenerate the most lovely soul in this city! Salvation is a divine work. Regeneration is a divine work. Conviction for sin is a divine work. The turning of men to God is a divine work. The making of men ready for heaven is a divine work. We learn that when we are on our knees before God. When we are out talking and moving among men, we may go a great deal on the doctrine of salvation by works, but when we are on our faces before God, our helplessness is borne in upon us, and then, with self-abnegation and a sense of our utter insufficiency, we humbly wait upon God for Him to do His work. And, mark it, when our attitude is right before Him, He always uses us to do His work.

Will we make this prayer in our text personal tonight? That is the crucial point that I must ask you to face. Will we make this prayer of our text, tonight, personal? "Wilt Thou not revive us again, that Thy people here may rejoice in Thee?" Will we make it personal? Do we wish for it to be personal? I am going to ask you that direct question, and I am going to ask you to answer it, and I beseech you to answer it in sincerity and truth. Is this our prayer tonight? For let us know full well that each one of us shall be a helper or a hindrance in this proposed work. All along we are one of these two things in Christ's work. I speak now to Christians. I speak to those who have named Christ's name, who know and profess His cause to love. We are one of these two things in Christ's work. We are either helpers or hinderers in giving salvation to the perishing around us.

Who hinders Christ's work? First of all, the idle Christian hinders His work. Christians are not made to be idle. They are not made to be dumb. They are not made for their lips to be sealed so that they give forth no testimony to the dying around them. Christians are made to be busy. Christians are left in the world to be active, to be active for Jesus Christ. The idle Christian, then, hinders the cause of God in the earth. O Christian, if thou art idle, thou art hindering somewhere the advance of the great kingdom of God. The idleness of Christians surely hinders the march of the kingdom of God. Call to mind those solemn words of Jesus: "He that is not with Me is against Me; and he that gathereth not with Me scattereth abroad." What does your heart say to that? Jesus cursed the fig tree because it was idle. It ought to have borne fruit, and it did not; therefore, He cursed it. Meroz of old was cursed because Meroz was idle. Meroz did not take up arms against the other tribes of Israel. Meroz did not lift up the black flag, and turn traitor to Israel. Meroz simply stayed at home and left her brothers to go out and fight the battle, and they went out and fought, and won, but with their victorious refrain there was mingled the refrain of the curse of the angel of God: "Curse ye Meroz, curse ye bitterly the inhabitants thereof; because they came not to the help of the Lord, to the help of the Lord against the mighty." The idle Christian hinders God's work.

Nor is that all. The Christian not right with God hinders His work, and this is a matter of unspeakable gravity, if only we rightly knew it. If he is not right in his outward conduct, we can see how that hinders God's work; but, brethren, what wounds the Lord Jesus Christ receives in the house of His friends, His real friends, from men who do love Him, men who, if they were crowded to the wall, would die for Him! And yet what wounds He receives at the hands of such men, full many a time, by their inconsistent words and their inconsistent works. How we hinder the cause of Jesus Christ ourselves! We need not trouble so much about the attacks of some blatant infidel out yonder, who rails against the Bible. That is not the supreme trouble at all, but the trouble supreme to the advancement of our Lord's kingdom in this world is with the people of His kingdom, with those who love it, and who are of it, and yet whose lives do not harmonize with it. There is our supreme trouble. If we are saying wrong things, or if we are doing wrong things; if, in our lives, inconsistencies may be seen; if there is marked worldliness, and if we fall so far short of the characteristics of what a Christian ought to have, so that men about us believe that our religion is just a theory, and not the dominating passion of our lives, then are we hindering the cause of Christ to a very sad degree.

Nor is that all. We hinder the cause of Christ, oh, so sadly, even though outwardly all may seem to be well with us, if inwardly it is not well with us. I do not know of any thought for the Christian more terribly serious than this—that the secret condition of his heart, which condition his wife does not know, cannot know,—nor his most intimate earthly companion; which condition is known only to him and to God, the secret condition of his heart, is helping men in this city heavenward, or turning them hellward. The secret condition of your heart, a condition where no other eye can look, save One, that secret condition is now helping men up, or dragging them down, even as you sit in this building tonight. If a man's heart be right with God, then one prayer prayed from such a heart will have more power with God and with men than a thousand years of praying if the heart be all wrong with God. No wonder, then, that David prayed, "O God, restore unto me the joy of Thy salvation." Not salvation, mind you. He had that, but he prayed, "Give me back again the joy of Thy salvation, and then I will teach transgressors Thy ways, and then sinners shall be converted unto God."

When a man is right with God, then there is power in his praying. When a man is right with God, he may lock the heavens, as did Elijah, or, like him, he may unlock them. Mind you, it is the supplication of a "righteous" man that availeth much. So the secret condition of our hearts is helping now, or hindering now, these appointed gospel meetings, and will help or hinder them all along. If there is one picture in the Bible more than another that is solemn in the extreme, it is the picture of Achan's secret sin, and the doom that followed, in Joshua's army, in the olden time, which sin was known only to himself and to God, until Achan was searched and exposed.

O brethren, I had this night rather be nailed up in my coffin and buried alive than to go through these gospel meetings with my heart all wrong, and my soul out of harmony with God; for I will either help or I will hinder others. Death were preferable infinitely than that a man should go on as a Christian, himself hindering salvation, himself hindering the blessed current of life that comes from God to man. Death were preferable to that. But every Christian is one of these two things—a hinderer or a helper. He is a channel through which God is pleased to send His grace and blessings to lost men, or he is a clog to stop up that channel.

Is this text our prayer tonight? "Revive us again"—do we pray it? Know this, dear friends, God has a blessing for us here, blessed be His name, if only we wish it sufficiently. There is a recipe for soul-winning effort given back yonder in the seventh chapter of Second Chronicles, the observance of which never fails: "If My people, which are called by My name, shall humble themselves, and pray, and seek My face, and turn from their wicked ways; then I will hear from heaven, and will forgive their sins, and will heal their land." Don't you see it? The observance of that recipe never fails, and never will. We shall have here a great blessing, brethren, if we will faithfully live out the truth of this one verse.

Are we going to be satisfied if Christ's people are not revived? Then they will not be. Are we going to be satisfied if men all about us are not convicted for sin, and by divine power turned to Christ? Can we be satisfied if that result does not come? Then it will not come. Any preacher who can complacently preach on, month in and month out, and year in and year out, without seeing men converted; who can preach on through all that, and eat heartily and sleep soundly, will not see many converts under his ministry. I tell you, it is a life and death business in which we are engaged. Any church that can sit with folded hands and be satisfied if men are not turned to God, that can be easy with such a condition, will not have men added unto her, whose testimony will be, "In that place I was turned unto God." Do we wish to be revived? We shall have a great turning to God here, blessed be His name, if we wish it enough.

May I take one moment more just to talk to you about your plain duty? O God, bear Thou in upon us tonight the realization of this thought: We are left here to speak to dying men and women and children, at every possible place, and in every possible way, concerning the saving grace of Jesus Christ. Shall I talk to you about such duty? You Christians are to remember that teaching school is incidental; pleading law is incidental; being a farmer is incidental. All these things are but mere incidents in the life that you are left here to live. The supreme thing for which you live is to point men to Christ.

Shall I talk to you about your responsibility? That is, indeed, a solemn question: "Am I my brother's keeper?" The answer must be that I am his keeper to the last limit of my ability to help him. And by just letting him alone; by simple neglect, I may become my brother's spiritual murderer. Yonder is a man, let us suppose, dying on the streets of Dallas tonight. You will see him as you go home. He is sick, or drunk and helpless. We will imagine that it is a cold and stormy night. The snow and sleet are falling fast. The man is helpless. He lies in the gutter, all unconscious, it may be, of his awful danger. You look upon him, and pass him by. You must leave him to that awful fate, and in the morning he will be dead. And in the sight of heaven his blood will be required at your hands. You have no right to leave your brother to such a fate as that. Here is a neighbor or a child, or a brother, or a friend in spiritual night, and he does not realize it. He is condemned under the law of God, and he does not apprehend it. He may be in eternity tomorrow, and he does not take it to heart. He is without God, and without hope, and without light, and without life, and without grace, and without salvation, and you know it. Leaving him alone, to die in his sins, with such knowledge in your possession, means that, going down the dusty way of death, his blood may be required at your hands.

Do you wish for God to revive you and this church and His people here just as He wishes to do it? Do you men and women here tonight wish Him to send you that quickening of conscience, that renewal of strength, that restoring of the joy of salvation, that will help you to do what He asks at your hands? Do you wish that? Do you wish a revival here, just like He wishes it? What say your hearts? Answer honestly, and we are ready to be dismissed. Every man and woman here who answers back from the heart, "Before God, I do, tonight, go on record, with His eye upon me, and in the sight of men, that I wish Him to come during these quiet meetings, and absolutely have His way with me and with these meetings," will now, in this solemn moment, quietly signify such wish by standing.

(During the solemn pause many quietly rose.) The preacher added: "Behold us, Lord, as our solemn wish is now recorded in Thy sight, and in each other's sight. From our hearts we would most fervently pray, 'Wilt Thou not revive us again, that Thy people may rejoice in Thee?'"

3
Trumpeting the Gospel

(An Anniversary Sermon)

From Paul's First Letter to the Thessalonians, the first chapter and eighth verse, this sentence is taken for our text:

"For from you sounded out the Word of the Lord not only in Macedonia and Achaia, but also in every place your faith to God-ward is spread abroad; so that we need not speak anything."

Paul is here paying a most remarkable compliment to the church at Thessalonica. We shall search in vain in all the Scriptures for a more delicate and beautiful, and yet worthy compliment than this paid by Paul to that old-time church. Paul's compliments were worth having. He was no fulsome flatterer. He was discriminating and just, sincere and true; and therefore the more beautiful and significant stands out this compliment that Paul paid that church. "You are a dynamic force for the gospel," said Paul. "You have made, and are making, an impression for it so wonderful that I do not need to say one word." Did you ever note a more desirable compliment?

Sometime before this Paul had gone from Philippi, where he had been assaulted, maltreated, beaten, into this heathen city of

Thessalonica. When he opened his lips to speak the wonderful words of life, there was a remarkable response right in the heart of that heathen capital. Men who served idols, men steeped in the lust of idolatry and in the basest forms of vice that enshrouded that city, heard this man tell about One who came from the Father's house to reveal the Father's love, and who gave Himself to break the shackles from men who would be disenthralled, and who would walk in the sunlight of truth and righteousness. And they believed that message, and from that hour they voiced it with their noble living. From that hour their lives were fundamentally changed.

You have noted, haven't you, what an eye Paul had for strategic places? He was a seer. He had the forecast of the first statesman of the world. He knew that what was done in a city was a thing not done in a corner, but everybody would hear about it and know about it, and feel it, according to whether it should be good or bad. He knew that, and he put that great heart and hand and brain of his on the city. As goes the city, so shall go the country and the whole land. The city is the nerve-center and the storm-center of civilization and of Christianity. If these cities are not saved, Christianity is lost and all is lost. If these cities are saved, the whole land shall be vocal with the songs of heaven. Paul knew that, and that statesman-like eye of his swept those cities of Europe and Asia, and his heart coveted those centers, those strongholds for God.

Let everybody keep his eye on the city. That little remote village yonder, far in the country place, away from the noise and confusion of the city, is vitally interested in what we do here in the city, and we must not forget this, nor must they. A road leads from that little village, or from that remote country schoolhouse to the city; and not only does the road lead here, but also the boy out there is coming here, and we shall contaminate him and damn him, or we shall disenthral him and add to his strength and nobleness, and send him back a joy to the old folks that sent him away with so much concern. The little remote country community is vitally interested in the city, interested in its laws, interested in it in every respect. There is no drawing a line and saying, "The city shall stay on this side." It isn't going to do it. "And the country shall stay on that side." It isn't going to do it. We are neighbors, and ever becoming more so, mingling and intermingling. We are to plan our deeds of noblest strength right in the heart of the city. Paul did that in Thessalonica, and in the other cities of the time in which he lived, showing what an eye he had for strategic situations.

Did you notice this expressive word that Paul employed? We come upon it here for the first time, and I think the only time in the New Testament, in its description of the business of a church: "From you sounded out the word of life." The church is to be God's trumpet. "From you is trumpeted forth the word of life." From this trumpet the word of life is to be sounded forth. A church is God's agency supreme in the world through which His love is revealed and His grace made known. That is the business of a church, and here it is strikingly set forth.

Let us look at two or three vital truths that are enwrapped in this compliment Paul pays to the church at Thessalonica.

And, first, he tells us the kind of men that sounded out the word of life. The context gives us the description of such men. They were men who possessed the fundamental virtues of the Christian life, the cardinal virtues, the vital virtues—three of them. "Remembering," said Paul, "without ceasing, your work of faith, your labor of love, and your patience of hope in our Lord Jesus Christ." These are the fundamental, Christian virtues, and these Christians in Thessalonica possess them. "Your work of faith, your labor of love, your patience of hope." What a trio that, and how fond Paul was of such trios! In concluding that incomparable chapter on love, the thirteenth chapter of First Corinthians, Paul said, "And now abideth faith, hope, love, these three; but the greatest of these is love." The abiding virtues, the cardinal virtues, the fundamental virtues in a Christian life, were possessed by these Thessalonian Christians, who sounded forth the word of life, about whom Paul spoke so glowingly.

And Paul further said, "You were possessed by these virtues; you did not receive the gospel in word only, but also in power, and in the Holy Ghost, and in much assurance." "That is to say," said Paul, "You were absorbed by these great matters; you took your religion seriously; you accounted it the first thing in the world to be true followers of God, to be faithful imitators of Christ." And still further, said Paul, "You held constant, you were invariable in the midst of sorest trials." Go read again in the book of the Acts, and see how those early Christians in Thessalonica were assaulted by the mob, how their blood flowed down their backs from the scourgings laid on them by cruel persecutors. Mark how they were hunted like the wild beasts on the mountains, how they watched, and yet as they watched, mark how they sang their songs of praise and voiced their hymns of obedience to Jesus! Paul said to those Christians, "You were constant in the midst of sorest trials; you did not recant when the battle became fierce; you did not flee, cowardlike, when the stress of the storm was on you; you were true." Oh, what a tribute was that for Paul to pay a little group of Christians, that they were constant, that they were invariable, that they obeyed without wavering! What a tribute was that—to the dependable man!

I have had occasion to say it before, but I would say it again and again—I care less and less for what you are pleased to term your brilliant man. I care more and more for your dependable man— the man true in every storm, the man who, when folks discuss him in their little circles and cliques and caucuses, must say, "You may put that man down as on the side of right though the heavens fall." Your dependable man, your man who is not a weather vane, your man who does not try to ride two horses at the same time going in opposite directions, he is the salt of the earth, the lifeblood of civilization. William Pitt made correct answer when one asked him one day, "Mr. Pitt, what would you pronounce the first qualification for a prime minister of Great Britain?" And he said, "The first qualification is patience." Said the questioner, "What would you pronounce the second qualification for a prime minister of Great Britain?" And Pitt replied, "The second qualification is patience." "Well, then," said the questioner, "what would you pronounce the third qualification?" And he said, "The third is patience." Wasn't it wisely said? We need patience to hold on, patience to plod, patience to persevere, patience to keep at our work without wavering or fainting. "Be thou faithful unto death"—not until death—that isn't what it says, that isn't what it means. "Be thou faithful unto death"—that is, die before being unfaithful. Any man ought to prefer any hour to die than to play the ignominious traitor and be unfaithful to the right thing. "Be thou faithful unto death"—die before being unfaithful—"and"—note the great promise—"I will give thee the crown of life." Now such were the men to whom Paul paid this incomparable compliment.

Notice here also the means that they employed for sounding out this Word of God, this gospel of life. The context explains that fully for us. First of all, the chief means for sounding out this conquering gospel was that such gospel produced in debauched lives the most marvelous transformations. There is nothing else in the world so moving, so startling, as for a man to be soundly converted by the gospel of God. These men of Thessalonica were converted all over, they were fundamentally changed. They had long served idols, but when Paul's gospel came in, breaking those idols into dust, presenting Jesus, the Way, the Truth, and the Life, the Emancipator of sin-driven men, the Life-bringer, the Hope-giver—when they heard that, they turned away from their idols to serve the living and true God, and to wait for His Son from heaven, whom He raised from the dead, even Jesus, who delivered us from the wrath to come.

There is nothing so wonderful as a true conversion, as for a man to be genuinely saved. We are hearing a great deal these days about all manner of prescriptions for advancing Christianity. They are telling us much, these days, about "socializing Christianity." I am shy of much of that kind of talk. The greatest thing in the world is for the individual man to be saved by the gospel, for such man to have a divine power to come into his life and turn him to God. That is the greatest thing in the world. The best advertisement for this gospel which we love is a saved man, living his religion. That is the supreme advertisement. Paul said, "You men are my advertisement; you are such a good advertisement I do not need even to speak anything." Did you ever hear of a more wonderful compliment than that? Oh, this is to be our glory, our predominant passion, to see men saved, to see men converted divinely by this glorious gospel, transformed, changed, saved!

I have told you before, I think, of the most remarkable conversion I ever saw. Will you bear with me while I tell you again about it? The occasion was several years ago, in a great outdoor Texas meeting. Conditions religiously were dreadfully hard and bad where such meeting was held. I think I never knew them worse. Men with white locks about their ears were lost, and even their grandchildren followed in forbidden and ruinous paths; and the few people of God in the community were down and beaten and defeated, it seemed. One of the causes for such conditions was that a group of men had had a series of little, pesky, religious debates; and the result was that conditions were hard and harsh and bad on every side.

All these things were recounted in the preacher's ears, as he began the meetings. I shall never forget the repeated story of the people there concerning one of their citizens, a man known for a radius of hundreds of miles. I could speak his name, but will not. He would not forbid it, for I could speak it to God's praise. They told me much about this same Big Jim. They said, "He will come to the meeting once this year; then he will curse you and the meeting out, and curse the churches, and then he will wait another year to come again. That is his style. You need not waste any preaching on him." They described him so that I could not mistake him—he was the largest man in all that section. One night I stood up to preach, and in came Big Jim. I shall never forget the emotions that then possessed me. Here was the chief of sinners, so the people said; what could be done for him?

That night I preached, and God's Spirit moved upon the audience mightily, and men with their white locks and stooped shoulders were, like little children, that night turned to the Savior. Grandfathers that night came, who had walked the wrong way for well-nigh their threescore years and ten. And their grandchildren also came. The Spirit of the Lord was upon us in marvelous fashion that night.

Yonder sat Big Jim like a granite shaft. And when that service was concluded, a little group of people stayed behind and talked with one another about the hour just past, as men are wont to talk over such an occasion. Ever and anon they would refer to Big Jim. They said, "He was here tonight, but he won't be back." One said, "I believe he will return; I never saw him look as he looked tonight." Another said, "No"; another said, "Yes." Presently after I had left the tabernacle to find the cottage where I slept, as I went along through the quiet woods, I heard someone talking in the darkness of the night. I did not mean to be an eavesdropper. There were two of them talking, oh, so earnestly. They were talking to God. This is what they were saying: "Mighty God, the people are saying that Big Jim is too much for Thee. Oh, break to pieces our unbelief, and let all this country know that God is Master of the situation, that He can save even the chief sinner here!" They said, "Master, we plead Thy promise to Thy disciples about two who may agree, and if agreeing concerning anything they should ask, Thou wilt hear. We agree that we want Big Jim saved for the glory of God, and to stop the mouths of gainsayers once and forever in all this section."

I quietly went my way, leaving them thus on their knees. They did not know that I had heard them, nor do I know who they were. The next day came and wore to evening, and again I stood up to preach, and in came Big Jim again. Yonder he sat at the rear of the tabernacle; and then I said, "Father, give me the word of life for this brother man."

I told the story of the prodigal son, that restless, wayward lad, who went away from home against the protest of love and wisdom's voice, and who went from bad to worse, and down and down, until yonder he is in the swine fields eating of the husks wherewith he fed the swine. One day the prodigal became homesick and soul-sick and he said, "I have missed it all; my whole life's course is a grim sarcasm; I have missed it all. I can do better than this as a servant in my father's house; and worst of all, worst of all, I have sinned against my best friend, I have sinned against my father who loved me, and I have sinned against my father's God. I will go back and I will tell him all." You know the rest. You know how the father, whose heart ached forever with an aching that would not stop because the boy was gone, looked one day and saw him coming, and while he was yet a great way off, that father ran to meet him and to fold that thing of rags and shame to his heart, while the boy wept and said, "Father, I did not come back to ask to be your boy, but to tell you that I have sinned against you and heaven, and that I am not worthy to be called your son, but ask only to have a servant's place." And the father said, "Kill the fatted calf for the boy returned; bring him the best robe; put on his finger the ring—emblem of love that never dies." That was what I preached. And then I said, "I bring you a gospel to which I have anchored my very soul; I am willing to die by it, and I am trying to live by it; I am going to meet God with it when I stand before Him in the judgment. I came one day and surrendered to that Savior whom God the Father sent. Is there a man here who will surrender to Him now?"

Big Jim started towards the preacher, and in a moment half a thousand men were seeing him and all these rose to their feet. Were they dreaming? Was it too good to be true? They were on their feet, looking, listening, sobbing. Down that long aisle came Big Jim, and when he reached me he caught my hand and said, "I put you on your sacred honor—will Jesus Christ save me if I give up to Him?" I said, "On my sacred honor, I answer that He will." And then he looked at me again while the men, who stood all about us now, were begging him to yield to Christ. He spoke again: "But you must remember that I am the worst man out of hell." I answered back, "My Savior died for the worst man out of hell, and He is able to save him now." Once more he looked at me and said, "When would He save me if I were to surrender myself to Him right now?" I said, "On the authority of Jesus Christ, on which I have rested my soul for time and eternity, I declare that He will save you right now, and you yourself may be the judge, if you will fully surrender to Him now."

Then he turned that great, bronzed face, pitiful in its anguish, up towards the heavens, and gasped this prayer: "Lord Jesus, the worst man in the world gives up to you right now!"

I cannot tell you all the rest. I don't know that the angels could tell it all. But God unloosed his tongue, and Big Jim witnessed for Jesus then and there as I never heard Him witnessed for before nor since. Old grizzled men came and kissed Big Jim; and old women came and kissed him; and little children kissed him, for the chief of sinners was saved. And then the word went to and fro as fast as the winds could carry it that God was in the midst of the people forgiving sin.

Gentlemen, one such apologetic as that for Christianity sounds out the gospel word both far and near as can nothing else in all the earth. We will stay by the simple, old-fashioned, supreme vocation of Christ's church, and that is to win men to God. That is the biggest thing in all the world. And when that is done, light will spread and darkness will flee, and righteousness will follow. That was the way the gospel of old was made victorious. Men were converted to God and others soon heard the gladsome news, and themselves were led to ask the way of life.

Then, again, these Thessalonians, by their lives, attested their profession. Their profession was vindicated by their lives. Paul said: "Your life has been so glorious, you have been such an inspiration, such a blessing, such an example to all the people throughout all Greece, north and south, that I do not even need to say a word in defense of the gospel. You are the gospel embodied, you are the gospel incarnated in lives, you are the gospel lighting up a house that was once inhabited by black evil things, and now shines to the praise of God." Their lives attested their profession.

Here is the best argument for Christianity: The right kind of a Christian—mark you, the right kind of a Christian. He is the one unanswerable, invulnerable argument for Christianity in this world—the right kind of a Christian. These men said, wherever they went throughout Greece, north and south, all through Macedonia, all through Achaia, wherever they went, they said, "We were debauched, we were bad, we were enslaved, we were handicapped by sin, we were depraved. We accepted Christ, and He changed our natures; we are now new men." And their lives said it much louder than anything their lips could say. That is the power of the gospel.

Oh, my fellow Christians, that is its irresistible power. You can feel some men, the Christian element in them is so strong. That was the glory of Phillips Brooks. You could not analyze his preaching, it is often said, but you could feel him. That was the glory of Robert E. Lee, that matchless man of Southern history. That was the glory of William Pitt, Prime Minister of Great Britain. That was the glory of Washington, Father of His Country. That is the glory of many a little modest man, and many a little shrinking woman, whose life is radiant with the sunlight of sincerity, and with a glorious enduement of God's goodness and truth and grace. These men of old thus lived their religion.

There was another thing that was conquering in their Christian character, and that was their faith was as clear as the sunlight, and as enduring as a granite mountain. Their faith—what a vital word is that! What a vital word that is for these times, with all the theological millinery we have about us, and all the fads and fancies, the cults and innovations! Their faith was as clear as the sunlight, as unshakable as Gibraltar. These men knew what they believed, and why, and they were able to give to every man they met an answer for that marvelous hope that illumined their way, and transformed their lives.

I would summon you today, my fellow Christians, to be clear in your faith. Know what you believe concerning the things of religion, and why. The man who speaks with the accent of sincerity and definiteness is the man of power. Remember the apostle's question: "If the trumpet give an uncertain sound"—(and remember we are trumpets for Christ)—"if the trumpet give an uncertain sound, who shall prepare himself to the battle?" Your testimony for God is to be clear and unhesitating and certain. Alas! that some Christians in their faith are like Reuben of old, unstable as water, and like him, too, it may be said of each of them: "Thou shalt not excel." Be clear in your faith. Don't be religious mugwumps. Jesus was the very Prince of dogmatists and His apostles after Him were to the last degree dogmatic in their faith. Listen to Peter: "Neither is there salvation in any other; for there is none other name under heaven given among men, whereby we must be saved." That is dogmatic. Listen to John, that disciple of love and gentleness: "Who is the liar, but he that denieth that Jesus is the Christ? This is the Antichrist, even he that denieth the Father and the Son." Listen to Paul: "But though we, or an angel from heaven, preach any other gospel unto you than that we have preached unto you, let him be accursed." And to increase the emphasis, he repeats it in the next verse. Oh, my fellow Christians, on this tremendous matter of religious faith we want to be as clear as the sunlight, and as unshakable as the everlasting hills. " 'Tis conviction that convinces."

Take Karl Marx. He is the most dogmatic and pronounced personality that Germany has produced in a hundred years—that noted socialist leader. Mighty passions and convictions and beliefs have surged in his life, and he has put the stamp of his forceful personality throughout all Germany and Europe, and the world. Certainly you do not agree and I do not agree with many of his teachings; but when a man with the passion and the conviction and the personality and the power of Karl Marx goes across the world, men will feel him. And there are ten thousand fires burning in human hearts today because Karl Marx believed something. And the world is studying this hour, in a way never before, the teachings of socialism, because Karl Marx believed something.

Take the Roman Catholic Church. She has two special dogmas, which, both in season, and out of season, she proclaims: The dogma of the church, and the dogma of the mass. We cannot in the remotest degree accept her teachings concerning the church and concerning the mass; and yet that great body concerning which I would not willingly say one improper or unjust word—that great body goes through the earth proclaiming that the church should be supreme in the regulation of all human conduct, in the home, in society, in things political, everywhere. You stand amazed, as do I, that such dogma should have advocates. And you are the more amazed at their other dogma that simple bread and wine are actually changed into the very body and blood of Jesus, their doctrine of transubstantiation, after the blessing of such bread and wine, by the proper ecclesiastic. And yet that mighty ecclesiasticism, through the centuries, has boldly taught these two dogmas, and has put the impress of such teachings in every land beneath the stars. They believe something—that explains it. I honor them, while utterly differing from them, for persisting evermore in urging those amazing dogmas, because they believe them.

And in the other days, when Martin Luther, that immortal Protestant, who before was a Catholic priest, came to believe the God-honoring doctrine that men are not justified by human works, nor by human righteousness of any sort, but that they are justified by faith in Jesus Christ, Luther went out and—aforetime a devout Romanist—Luther went out and proclaimed the doctrine of justification by faith in such a way that he wrested Germany from the hands of the Pope, and thrilled the world with his mighty pronouncement of Protestantism. He believed something, and he avowed it. When he had determined to go to the Diet of Worms, and men tried to keep him from going because he would go in the face of probable death, together with every threatened punishment, he answered them back: "If there were as many devils as there are tiles on every roof in Württemberg, I can but go and say what my soul knows to be true." He believed something.

My fellow men, let us have a faith that does not change with every change of the moon. John Knox put his marvelous personality on Scotland and on every other land beneath the sun because he believed something. He rescued Scotland from the grip of unbelief because he believed something. And John Knox's daughter, Jane Welch, when they offered her her husband's freedom if he would recant, answered like this: "I would sooner have my husband's severed head brought me in a charger than for him to deny the things he has taught and believed." Oh, for a generation of great believers!

But there was another all-important thing about these early Christians. They attested their faith by their deeds. They proved their religion by their works. They vindicated their hope by their deeds. That is the apologetic that we must have—just that. All my time could be spent on that one simple point. But I leave it after referring to just one incident in the life of David Brainerd. That Christly missionary to the Indians, when he became so old and weak and crippled with rheumatism that it seemed that there was nothing else that he could do but wait there in his little hut and die, was found one day kneeling on the floor, too feeble to sit in his chair, teaching a little Indian girl her A B Cs. And men said, "What! Has it come to this? The great David Brainerd down on the floor teaching a little Indian girl her A B Cs!" And he said, "Happy if with my latest breath I may but be permitted even to teach a little Indian girl her A B Cs."

You will make the application, won't you, of this old-time text? Every church, I remarked in the beginning, is to be a trumpet for Jesus Christ—to voice the word and love of Jesus Christ. My beloved people here of this flock, you will make the application. The church at Thessalonica was inevitably situated to influence many people. How like your own! Thessalonica was a city of telling commerce. How like your own city here! The roads were many that came and went to Thessalonica. How like your own! And the blows struck for Jesus Christ yonder in Thessalonica sounded out throughout all the province of Macedonia. Even so, a light here properly given will send its rays far and near. A testimony here properly given will go far beyond your own circles. Like Paul, who was a patriot, as every man ought to be, you can say today, "I am a citizen of no mean city." And by reason of that very position that you have, you are called upon to sound out the word of life, of righteousness and truth in every blessed and glorious way.

God has providentially thrust you into an exceedingly responsible place. Do not shrink from it. Oh, certainly there are times when you want to flee to the woods never to come back, but you can't. God has providentially thrust you into the gaze of the people, far and near, and you are called upon all the more to witness worthily for Jesus Christ. Here in Dallas are several of our denominational boards. Here is your State Mission Board doing the largest state mission work in all the world. Here also is your Woman's Work, in its official organization. Here also is your Young People's Board. Here is your denominational paper. Here is your great sanitarium. Then God has given us this noble church, with her more than two thousand members. What a host of people! And your fear sometimes is as mine, that this church will be a hospital of people not active, instead of a barrack of soldiers aggressive for God.

And then think of the army of strangers within our gates. I have often wondered if our ministry to the strangers is not broader than our ministry to our own homes and firesides; for scarcely a day passes that some stranger near or far does not write to give grateful testimony to the blessing brought him in this worship with us here. By all these facts we are called upon to be the right kind of men and women. Then see our various church agencies of this one church. See the Sunday school, the supreme opportunity of the church. To save a boy is an incomparably bigger thing than to save a man. To save a girl is more important than to save a woman, for you save a life as well as a soul when you save a child. Here too are our organizations for our hosts of young people. Here too are the multitudes of women with their many and mighty forces. There is nothing more pitiful than for a woman saved through the blood of Christ to have her energies diverted into some little, narrow shallow channel of selfishness, to gratify some small, passing impulse. Some time ago a cultured woman came to her pastor, not in Dallas, I am glad to remark, to say there was a Buddhist lecturer in the city, and to ask if the pastor would not let the Buddhist lecturer have the pulpit from which to exploit Buddhism. The pastor was amazed beyond all speech, and said so, that a woman, given her position in this country, of happiness and honor—given such position by Jesus Christ—would wish her pastor to offer his pulpit for the exploitation of Buddhism, when a woman in Buddhist countries slavishly waits on her husband, is not worthy to eat at the same table with him, gets such crumbs only as he chooses to give, and is taught that she does not have any soul at all. What a tragedy it is when a woman, whose chief charm is her religion, is diverted from her church life into little, shallow, narrow channels of thought and activity. What a tragedy when her life is taken up with religious cults and fads and isms, and the deep practical things of Christianity are forgotten.

I summon the Christian women who are here today, given their incomparable position by the blood of the Son of God—I summon them to give their best to Jesus Christ and to His church. And these men, these saved men, I summon them to give their best to Jesus

Christ and to His church. My fellow men, if Jesus Christ loved the church enough to die for it, you and I surely ought to love it enough to live for it. There are two great organizations in the world—there are not many that are worth a great deal; there are two that are absolutely invaluable, the home and the church. If you and I are to plant our labors in life where they will count for the most, then let us consecrate our best labors for the home and for the church. The home has been wretchedly neglected. I might mention a host of agencies at work for the redemption of children that would have been made unnecessary by the right kind of homes. The church also has been sadly neglected.

It is a day of organizations now. Sometimes I have wondered if some men could find enough space on their coats to put all the buttons of the various organizations to which they belong. I have not a word of railing to say against such organizations, but I would say, my fellow Christian men, that in these short lives that you and I are to live, we ought to link our lives with those organizations that will count the most, and with the organizations that are of most vital value to a needy world. Let us invest our lives, our love, our money, our service, not so that the fruits and influences therefrom shall be evanescent like some passing cloud of the morning, but so that they may abide through all the coming years and forevermore. I summon you to give your best to Christ, your best to Christ today and always.

I have been with you many years. Oh, I know the stress and the travail of the preacher's life. I have gone to my room a thousand times and asked God if I might be released from it all; and then the instant the words escaped my lips I have hastened to say, "Nay, Lord, nay, only give me grace to be the preacher I ought to be!" Every waking hour I sing:

> Happy if with my latest breath,
> I may but speak Thy name;
> Preach Christ to all, and gasp in death,
> Behold, behold the Lamb.

My grandfather was a preacher through the long, long years. In his last illness his affliction was such that he could not lie on his bed

for one moment for many days. But people came to him for a re-
gion of forty or fifty miles, and there sitting in his chair, with his last
expiring breath, he preached Christ Jesus, the world's one and
only, but all-sufficient Savior. I should like to go like that to the last,
to the last, witnessing for Jesus. O my fellow Christians, I summon
you to give Christ your best of love, of service, of life. His is the
most virile, the most masculine, the most heroic, the sublimest business on earth—the making of His gospel victorious everywhere.
Give Him your best, your best, your best, forevermore.

O my fellow Christians of this church, a church dearer to me
than my heart's-blood, God knows—my fellow Christians of this
church, I summon you anew today to give your best to Christ; to
be done with all playing at your religion; to be done with all luke-
warmness. I summon you to come with the red, rich blood of
human sympathy for all mankind, for good and bad, for high and
low, for rich and poor, and give your best to win this city and state
and world to Jesus, so that you may hear that plaudit which it were
worth worlds at last to hear, "Well done, thou good and faithful servant."

4

A New Testament Good Man

For he was a good man, and full of the Holy Ghost and of faith: and much people was added to the Lord (Acts 11:24).

This is Luke's description of Barnabas. A name is often the mirror of the nature behind the name. Barnabas means "the son of consolation." This name was given him by the apostles to indicate the kind of man that they esteemed him to be, and that he really was. Luke's description of Barnabas is one of the briefest, and yet, at the same time, one of the most comprehensive ever given concerning any life. "For he was a good man, and full of the Holy Ghost and of faith: and much people was added unto the Lord."

It is the Bible portrait of one of the most useful men of which the Scriptures give any account. "He was a good man, and full of the Holy Ghost and of faith." This word "good" employed here by Luke is not accidentally employed. It is the very word that Luke meant to use. When he characterized Barnabas as a good man, he meant exactly what he said.

You search in vain in the Bible for many tributes as high as is this tribute paid by Luke to Barnabas. The Bible is very careful about

its tributes to men. Now and then there are the outflashings of com-
mendation and of approval, of splendid tributes to men in the Bible,
but yet not as many as you might at first suppose. Exceedingly careful is the Bible about the use of this word "good," as applied to any
man or to any thing. Luke, however, did not misuse it. He meant
to use this word, and it is exactly the right word.

We are very careless about our use of that word "good." It is a
very strong word, and should not be hawked about with careless,
indiscriminate use. We often talk about a "good man," when he
comes far short of being a good man. And the world talks about
"good fellows," meaning, maybe, that they are genial, or that they
treat people to a cigar; or something a good deal more hurtful than
a cigar; meaning that they are hale fellows well met, and not
meaning good in any blessed sense at all.

Luke, when he uses the word "good" with reference to Barnabas, uses the right word. He did not mean, to be sure, that Barnabas was a perfect man. He would have badly missed it if he had
made any such claim for Barnabas. We read further along in the
story of this man Barnabas how he missed perfection quite badly.
You recall that he and the noble Paul had a "sharp contention" one
day. Hot words followed. I do not know which was to blame—perhaps both. It is generally that way. When there is a serious difficulty,
generally two people are to blame instead of just one. At any rate,
in this case, sharp words were spoken by these two men. It was a
"sharp contention," so the Scriptures describe it, and then they
parted asunder, one going his way, and the other his. So there is the
revelation of the fact that this man was not any perfect man. The
Bible does not make any such claim for any man. It distinctly re-
pudiates that claim. "If we say that we have no sin, we deceive ourselves, and the truth is not in us." "There is not a just man upon the
earth that doeth good, and sinneth not." But when the Bible
speaks of a good man it looks at the tenor of his life, at the great,
absorbing, all-controlling drift and tendency of his being, and
with that view Barnabas measured up nobly, for he was a good man.

The Bible speaks of David as a man "after God's own heart."
Did it mean that he was perfect? Alas! it meant nothing of the sort.

He was far from perfect. Three of the most fearful crimes in all the catalogue of crimes are laid at the door of this man David. He was a traitor. Can there be anything much more heinous than to be a traitor? David was a murderer. The blood of another man's hands was on his own. He was an adulterer. Treachery, murder, adultery! These three black crimes, so closely linked with one another, were laid at David's door. Did the Bible mean to indicate that he was a man without blemish or sin? Nothing of the sort. It meant that in David's life, taken as a whole, there was a struggle and an inclination after the good, and despite the fearful sins into which he was so suddenly plunged, indescribably awful, David did feel out after the good, and after the will of God. And you will make a fundamental mistake in studying the life of David if you leave out of it his incomparable confession in the Fifty-first Psalm. Never has there been penned a confession of sin as deep as that in the Fifty-first Psalm. Note some of its utterances: "Have mercy upon me, O God, according to Thy lovingkindness: According unto the multitude of Thy tender mercies, blot out all my transgressions.

"Wash me thoroughly from mine iniquity, and cleanse me from my sins. For I acknowledge my transgressions: and my sin is ever before me. Against Thee, Thee only, have I sinned, and done this evil in Thy sight.

"Purge me with hyssop, and I shall be clean: wash me and I shall be whiter than snow. For Thou desirest not sacrifice; else would I give it: thou delightest not in burnt offering. The sacrifices of God are a broken spirit: a broken and a contrite heart, O God, Thou wilt not despise."

There never was a confession penned in the world that was as deep as is the confession of David in this Psalm. So you will altogether misinterpret the real character of David if you do not include him in the Fifty-first Psalm. The Bible nowhere means to intimate that any man is sinless in the flesh. Luke does not mean it here.

Luke goes on after employing this word "good" with reference to Barnabas, and pictures his character still further: "He was full of the Holy Ghost and of faith." This indicates his spiritual intensity— "full of the Holy Ghost." "Full," that is, he was God-possessed. He was filled with the divine Spirit. And that explains the spiritual life that he lived, as it was crowned with noble deeds. Have you sometimes seen a noble riverbed, wide and deep, and yet the drought has come, and the water has become lower, and the stream is narrower and thinner, and all along in the riverbed trash accumulates, and evil things hide and lurk? What a picture is that of the religious life largely devoid of the Spirit of God. And then have you seen that riverbed filled with water? The heavens have emptied their abundant rains, and the waters have accumulated and gathered until that great bed is filled to overflowing, and all the accumulated trash is swept before that mighty stream, as it rolls on to the sea. That is the picture of Barnabas. He was full to overflowing of the Holy Ghost. Men may today be full of the Holy Ghost just as Barnabas was. Men may have, and ought to have their lives guided and dominated today by the Spirit of God as really as did Barnabas. It is all a mistake that God's people may not have the guidance and the power of the Holy Ghost today, even as they had it in the olden time. I do not speak, of course, of the unusual signs that were sometimes in the Spirit's workings, in the apostolic times, but I do speak of the vitally essential fact of the Spirit in the Christian's life to give guidance and wisdom and light and power and strength. Without His help, all our work is utterly futile. We may daily have His help if we rightly ask for it.

Barnabas was also full of faith. The Lord Jesus Christ was no empty abstraction to Barnabas. He was no visionary, far-off theory. Jesus was real to Barnabas. He looked to Him to save him, and then he looked to Him to be the inspiration and guide of his whole life. Christ was gloriously real. His claims were real, His purposes in the world were real. The conquering power of His kingdom among men, these all were vitally real to Barnabas. He was "full of faith," as well as "full of the Holy Ghost." And men of heroic faith move the world. Abraham was a man of such faith. Sitting yonder under the oaks of Mamre, Abraham was the mightiest man of his time, because he implicitly believed God. Paul was a man of such faith, and no man about him could compare with him, because he believed God. Since Barnabas was a man "full of faith," as well as "full of the Holy Ghost," you are prepared for Luke's further statement: "Much people was added unto the Lord." Given a man with such a character, with such a basis, and you are prepared for the result, "Much people added unto the Lord," as the outcome of his labors.

And, now, let us look a little more carefully to see the evidences, the fruits, the proofs, that Barnabas was the good man, the spiritual man, that Luke describes him to be. What are these fruits? There are several that appear right on the surface of the Scriptures.

Here is the first: Barnabas was a man of the noblest generosity. That is our first introduction to him. Back there in that remarkable meeting that was sweeping the Jerusalem church, and in which Barnabas was brought to Christ, the very first revelation we have of this man Barnabas was an expression of the noblest generosity of which he was capable. The Scriptures say that having land, he sold it and brought the price thereof and laid it down at the apostles' feet, and joined himself from that hour to the company of believers, and from that hour went out a poor man, like Paul. Surely that is a practical evidence that he was a good man? It will pinch him to be a good man at all. Can a miserly, stingy, penurious, hard-fisted man be a good man? Won't it drive him to the last ditch to begin to make such a claim as that? He may be clever. He may be smart. He may be witty. He may be aggressive. He may be influential. He may be powerful. But is he a good man? So the very first fruits, the very first intimation of the character of this man Barnabas is voiced in Luke's description, given in the fourth chapter of Acts, of his noble expression of generosity in the gift of his goods to the cause of Christ. I pause on that a moment more. The bondage of money is the most selfish bondage that ever puts its grip on the human heart. There are fearful expressions of bondage otherwise; the bondage of some awful habit, the bondage to lust, the bondage to this thing or that, fearful expressions of bondage here and there, as you can think of them now. But the most galling and selfish of all the expressions of bondage the world ever heard of is the bondage to money. Oh, I tremble for every Christian that I ever see rapidly making money! Nor do I stop at trembling. God is my witness. As a matter of conscience, I pray for every such person, that he may not be drowned with the love of money, for it is the root of every kind of evil in the world. This man Barnabas was a man that mastered his money, and any man who masters his money is the master of the situation. Any man whose money masters him is the most fearful slave that today cringes before any altar in the world. And, remember, a man may be mastered by a few hundred dollars as well as by a million. A man with just a few hundred dollars is often pulled around by the nose just as really as the man of millions.

It was a most meaningful thing when, years ago, in one of the large churches, somebody sent from the audience a little note to the preacher, saying: "The prayers of the church are desired for a young man in the congregation who is rapidly making money." There could not have been a more timely prayer offered in that congregation.

Years ago, when one of the large Eastern merchants sent his ships on the high seas carrying the commerce for the nations, one ship was due on a certain day, and did not appear, carrying $40,000 worth of goods. The merchant found himself restlessly pacing the floor, with the cold perspiration on his forehead, so anxious was he about that ship. Day after day passed beyond the time for its arrival, and no tidings came, and he was in an agony about it, until one day it dawned upon him: "I am a slave to my money. I am now in abject bondage to it." And then the fearful revelation shocked him to the depths, whereupon he sat down immediately and wrote out for the noble causes and institutions of his city his checks for $40,000, the amount of goods on that ship, saying: "I discover that my money is actually my master. From this hour I will master it, by the grace of God."

A man who can master his money has gone a long way towards the right mastery, and a man right about this question of money is likely to be right or easily led to do the right on every other question of religion. A Christian man wrong on the question of his money is likely to be seriously wrong on every other question in religion. Now that is putting it strongly, but I do unhesitatingly believe every word I am saying, and I would have these younger men, as well as the older ones, today to lay it to heart. A man right on the question of his stewardship to God, with his material possessions, is likely to be right on every question that comes up in his religious life. But the man wrong there is likely to be warped and distorted and wrong everywhere in his religious life. I pray you, then, to see that vital lesson that flashes out here in the life story of Barnabas. Oh, how I thank God for the exhibitions here in our own congregation, from time to time, of the mastery that men in this congregation have over their material possessions! It seems as easy for some of you to give as to drink water on a thirsty day. You are growing in grace and enlarging in the noblest things of the heart. But I must not tarry longer on this good showing that Barnabas makes on giving.

Here is another. He was a missionary to the core. When the news came that the Gentiles were being converted, the Jerusalem church sent Barnabas down to Antioch to see about that strange thing. You must remember that in the beginning these Jewish Christians had short-sighted visions. They believed in the Jew, and did not believe in anybody else. They had narrow views, believed that they were the people of God; and besides them there were no others. So the news came of a great work of grace down in Antioch, an alien community, and this church said, "Barnabas, you might go down and see about it." And, so, Barnabas went down, and the Scriptures say that when he came he saw the grace of God doing its work, and he rejoiced. Nor did he stop at that. The Scriptures say that he began exhorting them, with all his might, to cleave unto the Lord. He was a missionary to the core. The missionary is not a selfish man. The missionary has the heart of the Savior of the world. The missionary's vision is not circumscribed. The true missionary sees every human being in all this great, wide world. Barnabas was a missionary. The real missionary cannot be a narrow man. His heart feels and prays and yearns and resolves, and would help humanity everywhere.

And, then, see again his devoted life to Christ's cause. Oh, he was apostolic in his work! Brethren, we must remember that there is such a thing as being apostolic in work as well as in doctrine. We talk about doctrine, and certainly that is good. The man who would be careless about the doctrine is a great fool, or worse than a fool. It matters what a man believes. The men who are great Christians are great in doctrine. They have a basis for their religious life. But there is such a thing as being apostolic in work as well as in doctrine. Our emphasis is not all to be put upon the fact that we are to be apostolic in doctrine. Are we apostolic in work? Do we put ourselves out in self-denying service for other people? Do we go forth laboring for Jesus, not esteeming our lives dear to ourselves? Do we labor to help others, not counting our own interests at all? Oh, let us be apostolic in work as well as in doctrine! Barnabas was that sort of a man.

And, still again, Barnabas, in his name, gives us another important indication of the blessedness of his life. Barnabas was a "son of consolation." He was true to that expression. Because he was true to it, the apostles surnamed him Barnabas, meaning "a son of consolation." Isn't that a fine phrase for you—"a son of consolation"? What genius a man has who has the genius of comforting and consoling the people! Christianity is vigorous consolation. Christianity means comfort to the people. Christianity is not an oppressive thing, taking the heart and the hope and the life and the peace out of men. Oh, it is just the opposite. It is to hearten and to inspire and to uplift the sons of men. What a genius, then, a good man has when he has the genius of consolation! He is the man needed both in church and in state. Oh, these pessimistic croakers in politics; what shall I say of them? They make us weary. These calamity howlers, these fellows who see the bottom dropping out of everything, these men who are always croaking and whining and grumbling: may their tribe decrease! The man who can put heart and hope into others, the man who can see the bright side of the cloud, the man who can lift up lofty visions and noble ideals for his state—there is your statesman, and there is your man to follow. The man who, when the people are down, has the genius of saying the right thing to them, the man who can transform a state with constructive consolation, he is the man to lead the people. Senator Brown did it in Georgia. When the old state lay withered and prostrate and bleeding at the close of the war of the states, that man of such remarkable common sense, and that man of dauntless optimism, stood up and largely transformed Georgia in the affairs of state.

The man with the genius for consoling in the noblest sense, how much such a man means in the affairs of church! Mr. Spurgeon said he had one blind man in his church, and now and then spells came over his church, as come over many a church, when the people's lips hung down, and when they whined and cried and groaned. Spurgeon said that on such occasions the blind man got up and said just the thing that went through his church like an electric shock, and brought them back to their senses. One day the blind man asked them if God was dead; he would like to know. One day he asked if Jesus had vacated the world and let Satan have it; he wanted to know. And with words like that, with a genius always for saying the right thing, he put heart and hope and spirit into the great church. Now, Barnabas had that same genius, after the noblest sort of fashion. Christianity is vigorous comfort. And one of the most beautiful designations, given far back before the coming of Christ, of Christ when He should come, was this: "The consolation of Israel." And one of the most beautiful titles given the Almighty is this: "The God of all comfort."

Barnabas teaches us here a lesson of priceless moment. He knew the word to speak in season to the man disheartened. He knew the word to say to hearten and to inspire and to give courage and strength, rather than the opposite. Have you paused to consider the power of words? Men can undo you with their words. They can take the heart out of you. They can take the blood out of you. They can lay you prostrate. Or they can lift you up and send you out, buoyant and leaping as a strong man to run a race, with their words. Let Barnabas teach us all at this vital point.

Then, we need to see, also, that this man Barnabas was absolutely free from the mean spirit of jealousy or envy. You remember when they started out on their missionary tours it was Barnabas and Saul—Barnabas first—but a little later Saul overshadowed him. Then it was Saul and Barnabas always after that. How did this man bear it? He was perfectly content to walk in Paul's shadow. He did not compare in ability with Paul, and he was perfectly content to be subordinate to Paul's superior leadership. There is not a single intimation of his jealousy towards this young and rising man, not one.

An envious man is a little man. You cannot make anything else out
of him. He is a little man. He may be smart. He may be clever, He
may be witty, and talk fluently, but he is a little man. An envious man
is a dangerous man. Paul was a tremendously great man, and Barnabas knew it, and Barnabas was the man to put Paul to the front
everywhere. Barnabas said: "I will play second fiddle gladly. God
made me to play it. Who am I to be mouthing about it? This man
is incomparably greater and stronger than I am. I will walk in his
shadow. I will reinforce him. I will make his work greater. I will do
for this man everything I can." Such a man is himself a mighty man
in the kingdom of God. It takes a great man to do that. And
along with Paul's name down the ages forever will be linked the
name of Barnabas.

Have you every thought what Paul might have been without
Barnabas? O Paul, probably the best friend you ever had, next to
Jesus, was Barnabas. Barnabas had that spiritual insight that discerned
God's man. Somebody speaks of it as the insight of the Spirit of
God. Barnabas had it. Barnabas tided Paul over his hard places. You
remember two occasions, especially, when Barnabas stood for Paul,
two momentous occasions in Paul's life. Paul had been converted
down on the Damascus road, and went at once to preaching, you
remember. After a while, he came back to the church at Jerusalem,
and those people were dubious of him. They were afraid of him. He
was a man who had made sore trouble for them. He had persecuted
the church. He had been a terror to them, and they were exceedingly afraid of him. Barnabas, with that spiritual discernment that
he had, said, "Come, brethren, this is God's man." Barnabas stood for
him. Barnabas got in behind him. Barnabas tided him over that
rough place. That is a man worthwhile. Oh, how valuable are
these men in a church, or women, who can discern the Christ in
people, and despite the things that are rather fearful, despite the
things that are rather objectionable, can stand for them and say:
"Here, Jesus Christ is in this person, and let us help him; let us
hearten him; let us lift him up!" Barnabas did that. And then you remember when the meeting came at Antioch, Barnabas got down
there, and the meeting was too much for him. It was too big a thing

for him. He could not handle it. But he said: "I have a man who can handle it. I have a man who can preach after a noble fashion," and away he went and hunted up Paul, and brought Paul down to Antioch, and there for a year stood behind Paul in that great Antioch revival, Paul preaching the gospel of the grace of God with such wonderful power. Barnabas knew, better than any Mason knows the Masonic spirit, that Christ's Spirit was in Paul. Great man, wasn't he?

If you find the remotest feeling of jealousy towards any man, get to your knees and stay there until it is banished forever. A man is a little man that can have one shadow of grief to come over him by reason of anybody's bigness or greatness or popularity or success. Barnabas teaches us at this point, as we are taught by no other, perhaps, in all the Word of God, except John the Baptist. You recall how the crowds followed after John. You remember how popular John was. How he did sway those people as they came to hear him! But after a while another came on the scene, even Jesus of Nazareth, and the crowd slipped away from John. Some of John's friends, it seems, intimated to him: "John, how about this? The crowds are leaving you. How about it?" You remember what he said: "He must increase, but I must decrease." There is a great man for you. "He must increase, but I must decrease. I am just a voice. I am just a forerunner. I am the one to get the things a little out of the way for the mighty coming of Himself. He must increase, but I must decrease." There is a mighty man for you. Barnabas was that sort of a man.

Long enough have I spoken. One more word. We cannot all be great men like Paul. None of us can. But we can be good men like Barnabas. We can be good men. O brethren, to be good men, that is the first thing in the kingdom of God! Genuine goodness—not cleverness, not smartness, not intellectuality, but goodness—that is the fundamental thing in the kingdom of God. We may not be great. We may not sway the multitudes. We may not have our pictures in the papers. They may not be writing editorials about us. But we can be good men.

Do you not feel this morning to pray, "Lord, whatever the cost to us, make us genuinely good men and women." Let us pray that prayer with all our hearts just now.

5

An Old Testament Good Man

Caleb, the son of Jephunneh (Josh. 14:6).

Our study last Sunday morning was "Some Lessons from the Life of Barnabas." Barnabas was the Caleb of the New Testament, while Caleb was the Barnabas of the Old Testament. Not much is said in the Scriptures about Caleb, and yet enough is said to put him before us as one of the most inspiring examples of Old Testament history. He stands before us as a man of much dignity, of unbending devotion to principle, with a faith and a courage and a conviction after the very highest fashion. We do well to study the examples in the Bible of men who have wrought nobly in the cause of God. Such character study will point us lessons of how we may serve God to the best advantage.

Let us look, then, at some very meaningful lessons connected with this life story today. And, first, what of the character of Caleb? Barnabas, as we learned last Sunday morning, was called "the son of consolation." Caleb may well be called the man of "all heart," and in the life story given of him in the Word of God there are certain manifestations that appear in the story that show how truly he might bear the name of Mr. Greatheart. See the outflashing where his cheerfulness is one of the marked expressions of his life. You search in vain in this life story of Caleb to find a single instance where he was pessimistic, or cheerless, or dejected at all; but rather, the opposite shines out from his life story all along. He is one of the sunniest characters in all the Bible. Caleb had the New Testament spirit, enjoined long afterward by Paul, when Paul urged, "Rejoice evermore." And when again he said. "Rejoice in the Lord alway, and again I say, rejoice," Caleb had caught that spirit most graciously, and throughout his eventful life he was the man whose disposition was one of uniform and glorious cheerfulness. It is a most valuable lesson to learn, dear friends. "The joy of the Lord is your strength." The dejected, moping, cheerless Christian, the one without joy, the one whose face indicates sorrow forever, is not the one who makes a gracious impression upon an unbelieving world. Caleb is a man, with all that hearty, cheerful, sunshiny life, to give men to understand how healthy and happy a thing it is for one to be a genuine Christian.

The manifestation of his heartiness of nature is also seen in the power he had to calm other people. You recall the report that the spies made when they came back from the land which they were sent to spy out for Moses. You recall the report they gave when they came back. Caleb and Joshua gave a gracious report. They did not minimize the difficulties at all. They said, "There are difficulties. The men are mighty. Their cities are well fenced. Their surroundings are such as to call for our earnest attention, but we are well able to overcome all the difficulties." That was their report. And then you remember the report of the other ten, their comrades. They gave an altogether different report. All the twelve agreed that it was a wonderful land, that it flowed with milk and honey, that the grapes of Eschol were not equaled by any other grapes, that everything about the land was inviting and glorious. But ten of them were overwhelmed with pessimism and unbelief. And when they had given their pessimistic report, all the people broke forth into wailing and whining, and dismay seized the whole congregation of Israel. And then Caleb stood up, this man of great heart, and calmed the whole crowd. He so spoke as to still them, at least for a season, in that time of dejection and gloom.

Here then is a vital lesson: The men who can tranquilize others are much needed men. They are of untold value to the world—the men who can tranquilize others. Almost any man can set other men by the ears. In a dozen sentences he can set men by the ears until they are ready to go at one another like untamed beasts. But the man who can tranquilize others, the man who can quell the spirit of the mob, the man who in state, in society, in the clashes that come with the classes, the man who can stand in their midst and still them, is a man of priceless value to any community. The man who can do that in a church, in the affairs of religion, the man who can quickly bring discordant and divided elements to fraternal and common standing-ground for all, is a man of great price in the church of God. The one who can do that in the family, with the little frictions that come in the family life, who can suggest the way for the amicable adjustment of such little frictions, that one does a priceless work in family life. Now, Caleb had that gracious power, the power of stilling others in the midst of tumultuous and unhappy experiences.

And, again, the manifestation of the great-heartedness of Caleb is seen in the fact that his whole life was filled with positive encouragement for other people. O my friends, the man who has the genius to encourage other people is the man this world is looking for and needs. The man who can put heart into men rather than take heart out of them—this world suffers and pants and languishes for such a man. Caleb had the noble genius for putting heart into men. There are men who have the evil genius of taking it all out. You can hear them for a dozen minutes and feel like you had been to a funeral or to something much worse. They can take the heart out of you. They can look at you in a way to make you feel a dozen years older. Caleb had the spirit of heartening men. He could send men out with a lofty, conquering spirit, and such a man is ever a man of invaluable moment in this world. When reverses come, when crops are bad, when business is dull, when collections go slowly, when health seems under its normal condition, the man who can step in then and put spirit and heart into the people, the man who has the genius to speak the word in season to them who are weary, he is a man that church, and state, and home, and society, and all classes and conditions most earnestly need. Caleb was that sort of a man.

And then he was a man to the last degree courageous in heart. When the ten gave their report, in which they dealt out the doleful story of the greatness of the giants in the land of Canaan, how large and mighty were their cities, what grasshoppers they felt themselves to be, the heart of all the people was ready to faint. Then Caleb stood in their midst and said, "Much that these ten men say is so. There are great men in the land we have visited, and their cities are large and mightily fortified, but we are well able to overcome them." Not only able, he said, but "well able" to overcome them. There is a man of the loftiest courage. Every one of us needs to cultivate the spirit of genuine and quenchless courage, for there is constant need of such courage in the daily battle of life that we must fight. There are so many reverses and surprises and disappointments that come in the conflicts of human life, that every man needs, like Caleb, to cultivate the fortifying quality of courage. Oh, how weary the world is of whining and of crying and of pessimism, and of discouragement! Every man needs to set himself, as did Caleb, to cultivating continually the noblest sort of courage for the battle of life.

See another striking element in Caleb's character. That was his conviction and fidelity to duty. Caleb was a man who dared to be in the minority. He was a man who could, without any blanching of face, go against the crowd. He was a man who had his anchorage thoroughly defined, and who adjusted himself in absolute obedience to the convictions his soul felt and knew to be right. He dared, therefore, to be in the minority. He dared, therefore, to go against the tumult of the crowd; and in that he exhibited one of the most commendable elements, and one of the most forceful, that can be in a man's character. Alas, what sacrifices of truth, and of principle, and of right, are made, because men do not dare to be in the minority! In the world of politics, how men trim, and cavil, and cringe, rather than go against the multitude. Caleb was a politician of the right sort, or rather, I should say, a statesman,—a man who could be in the minority today, because the minority was right, and who could patiently wait for tomorrow, because ever is truth vindicated in due time. In society, in life's social relations, how many things are tolerated that people in their better natures rebel against. And yet they do not squarely abide the majority and say: "I will have no lot nor fellowship with this thing." One said to me recently, "I am ashamed every time I go through a certain social performance in this city." I replied, "Well, aren't you ashamed enough to turn the other way? Why yield pliantly to the spirit of the majority? Why not turn straight about, live honestly, be on good terms with your conscience, and squarely, with eagle-eye, face the things that are wrong, and with courageous hand push them utterly aside?" Caleb was a man who could stand out against the majority, looking to the revelation that the truth would have tomorrow and to the victory it would have. Ofttimes the majority is utterly wrong. That "The voice of the people is the voice of God" is ofttimes not so. Ofttimes the minority is right. And a man in the minority, with the consciousness that he is in alliance with truth and principle, must be a man who, for no cause, would give up his convictions of right and truth and duty. Athanasius uttered the pronouncement, "I, Athanasius, against the world"; and the stern theologian made the world hear and respect him.

Martin Luther went, against all the protestations of his friends, to the Diet at Worms, when they said, "It means your death." And Luther said, "I would go and declare what my soul knows to be right, if every tile on every roof in Württemberg were a devil." He won because he was true to principle. And Calvary, on which hanged the Son of God, is the crowning expression of the truth that the minority is ofttimes the sublime winning force because it is right. Here, then, is an element in Caleb's character, priceless and powerful—his fidelity to duty against the majority.

Note again that Caleb was a man who was perennially young. That is one of the most beautiful things in his life story. Here was a man who never did get old. Now, at the advanced age of eighty and five years, he said, "I am as ready to go to war as I was forty-five years ago. I am just as strong for it, and I am as ready for it. I am as eager for the battle as I was back yonder at life's middle time."

So there gleams out in the brief story of Caleb the delightful
thought that he was a man who lived to the last breath of his life,
young in spirit, and ever enthusiastic in his work. This is one of the
most beautiful exhibitions of Caleb's remarkable character. You notice him at this advanced age of eight-five years asking Joshua for
the hardest job in all the kingdom. "Let me go up yonder and conquer Hebron, that city in the mountains, fortified so well and surrounded by the sons of Anak, those giants we heard about years ago.
Let me have that hard task, and I will go and drive them out, even
as Moses promised me forty-five years ago." And Joshua allowed
him to go upon that difficult mission. A man is already an old man
who talks about "being let alone, having done his part." No man
must talk like that in this brief and important life. A man's face must
be set like a flint towards doing his duty, until the last breath shall
expire from his body. I say it today, from my heart of hearts, the very
hour that I cannot heartily work for God, that hour I want to go
home. There is not any place, there is not any need for any man
ever to get old in this world. And if a man will link himself with
the right things, and have the right view-point in the life he
lives, he will never be an old man.

Moses was one hundred and twenty years old when he died,
but the Scriptures tell us that his eye had lost none of its brightness,
nor was his natural force in any wise abated, and the reason is not
hard to find. Moses had the right view-point for his life. Moses was
linked with the right things. Moses had his anchorage first of all to
God, and accepted the central truth of the Christian religion,
that a man whom God has saved belongs utterly to God, to live or
to die, to say here or to go hence, according to God's will.

Nor was that all in Moses' case. Moses linked himself with great
causes for the lifting up of his oppressed fellows. Moses lived not a
day for himself. Why should he? Moses was not concerned about
his own ease or aggrandizement. Why should he be? Life is missed
in its sublime meaning if any man lives for himself. Moses gave himself as a servant, with his marvelous powers of brain and heart, a servant to lift up poor, beaten, oppressed Israel. And Moses in
self-forgetting sacrifice laid his life on the altar for the restoration

of Israel to her proper place among the nations of the earth. No wonder he was still a young man when he died. You take men who live like that, and they are not old men. Glorious spectacle was that of Gladstone, beyond eighty, with an eye yet bright, and with a mind well poised and keen and clear. Gladstone was linked with everything in the world that would make for the uplifting of humanity. And a man who thus links his life is not a man ever to get old. Caleb was perennially young, and at the advanced age of eighty and five Caleb asked for the hardest job that was ever given him in his life. "Let me have Hebron," he said. Hebron meant difficulty. Hebron meant battle. Hebron meant most exacting work. Hebron meant awful conflict. Hebron meant a fight to the finish. But there, at the advanced age of eighty and five, he said, "Put on my shoulders the hardest thing I have ever had to do, and I will go forth to the battle." And forth he went and won, to the everlasting credit of his name.

Oh, how stimulating that record is! Do you wish to make the most of life? Then do not seek the soft, easy places of life. Why should it matter to me if there should come home to me today the conviction that God would have me betake myself to dark and besotted Africa, to give myself in unstinted devotion to lifting up that race? Why should I halt a moment? I am not mine own, nor is a single power I possess mine own. I am God's. Why should I not adjust myself to what He asks, I in my sphere, and you in yours? If you would make life truly great, great in its deepest and highest sense, get the view-point Caleb had, and look not for the easy and soft places in life, but look for the places where you can have full opportunity to put every power of your nature on the altar for God, in the high service of humanity. Here is where many Christians fail. I haven't a question that many preachers largely fail because they are looking for easy and soft places. The one thing we are to think about, to care for, is that we may stand in the battle's front and in the thick of the fight, every man where God wants him, whether lawyer, doctor, minister, teacher, banker, farmer, or what not. If God has hard tasks and big jobs, and gigantic undertakings, let each one give himself to them with the spirit of Caleb, scorning easy places, asking for God to give him anything He wishes, in His infinite wisdom and love.

I speak to men here today, a large company, and very few of them with gray hairs, but we will have them after a little if we live. Let us address ourselves to life's problems as did Caleb. Let us make up our minds that we will never admit for a breath to ourselves that suggestion of the devil, that we have "done our part." Done our part! Done our part in life! Why, if we should live ten million years, and give every moment to the service of God, every drop of our blood, every thought of our brain, we would then have barely made a start in giving to God that which He so rightfully deserves at our hands. Let Caleb teach us. Let him teach us how always to be young. I know some old men, and you do, too, as the world counts it, that are not old at all. They are as young as lads of twenty-one. They are linked with great causes. They are forgetting themselves. They hear the heartbeat of a suffering world. They plan and they give, and they love, and they go, and they serve, forgetting self. They will never get old, but like Caleb they will come down to the end at last with perennial youth.

But see again Caleb's case. Caleb "wholly followed the Lord his God." That is what the Scriptures say again and again about him. And that is the secret, the sublime secret, of all the other wonderful elements of his character we have been considering. Caleb wholly followed the Lord his God. Whenever a man does that, what does he care for the clamor of the multitudes? Whenever a man does that, what does he care for the view of the majority? Whenever a man does that, what does he care for anything except the "Well done" of the God whom he serves? Caleb wholly followed the Lord his God. Caleb said that for himself: "I have wholly followed Him." And Moses said it about Caleb. And God Himself said, "My servant, Caleb, has wholly followed Me." So that he had the testimony overwhelming of the reality of his devotion to God. Now, in that fact resides the sublime secret of Caleb's marvelous power for God. And just there is the pivotal point upon which is determined man's relation to God and his relation to man. Here is where men are undone. If men do not follow God definitely and wholeheartedly, if men do not follow God, putting the reins of their lives into His hands, then such men make practical shipwreck of Christian usefulness and Christian joy.

Brethren, the supreme peril to us all is that we take our religion too easily. Our religion is not some nice bandbox affair. Our religion means battle and suffering and service. Our religion means the forgetting of self. Our religion is to soothe the brow of every aching head, and to give glad cheer to every cheerless heart, and to lift up every fallen life. The constant trouble is that we take our religion too easily. Caleb's spirit is the spirit for us all—wholehearted devotion to God. Oh, for that spirit, which found its expression in Paul, which found its expression in Luther, which found its expression in Wesley, which found its expression in Knox, which found its expression in Spurgeon, which found its expression in David Brainerd. Brainerd said, "I had rather win one poor lost soul for Christ than to win mountains of gold and silver for myself." That is the spirit that will consume the evil of the world and take away its chaff and make life a great and sublime thing. That is the spirit Caleb had, and that is the spirit for us all.

I do not wonder that many Christians get so little out of religion. The explanation is at hand. They put so little into it. I do not wonder that most of the time they stumble along in the dark. They live in the dark. I do not wonder that all along they are swept with conflicting emotions. They put themselves where such emotions can have the fullest sway. The Christian life is not to be lived in the twilight. The Christian life is to be open and above-board, and straightforward, and definite, and pronounced. The man who lives that sort of a Christian life reaches up any time with his hand and touches the hand of Christ. Caleb lived that sort of a life. O friends, if you would have power in your family, where some are gainsaying and ungodly, if you would have power in life's social relations or business relations, as you touch elbows with men, then yield never one iota to the admission of the wrong thing into your life. Stand like Caleb, with wholehearted devotion unto God.

Just here, I say, is the explanation for a thousand ills in human life. I talked yesterday at length with a strong businessman, upon whom troubles have recently come with terrible force and fury. Years ago, when I preached in another place, he found Christ and nobly confessed Him. Now he is down in the dark and deep valley of distress. He said, "I have come a long distance to go over this matter with you." I said, "The physician must diagnose his case before he is willing to give any medicine. Now, answer me, first, some questions honestly, and we will go over the whole matter." And when I probed the man with questions, I could not find that he had one religious habit in his life which he lived up to with a day's consistency—not one. He said, "Why, I see after my business on Sunday, and I have not read my Bible for months, and I go to church with awful irregularity, and I can hardly tell you when I did go alone and get down and utter a prayer." I said, "You have come this distance to ask me to tell you the trouble. You do not need that I tell you that you have trifled with your profession, and are trifling with your Savior, and are trifling with your church, and are trifling with the Scriptures, and are trifling with everything holy. You want to know why you have doubts? You have only to use your mind a second to find out. You want to know why you have no peace and no joy? You want to know why the joy of those other years is all gone—that zest, that interest in religion? The answer is right at your side. There is no conscientious devotion in your life to God, nor will you have those bright, blessed days again until you play the man for the Almighty."

Oh, my brethren and friends, God is my witness, there never passes a day that the most fervent prayer of my soul for you is not offered that you may wholly follow God! Oh, I grieve, beyond what you can know, to see you living any double, half-hearted life. I grieve to see you missing that steadfast joy, and that Christian power, that can come only to the men who walk as Caleb walked, who are straightforward and pronounced, and who give the benefit of the doubt always to God, and never to themselves. It comes to me again and again what a brother said some time ago in this church, that for a long while he just had enough religion to make himself thoroughly miserable, to give him a kind of a toothache feeling. You know exactly what he meant. He was living a half-hearted life. There is the explanation of 10,000 troubles in the Christian life. Men do not wholly follow God. Let Caleb teach us at that vital point, for here is the real secret of his masterful life.

The hour is past. You will indulge me this other word. What was the result of it all in Caleb's life? God gave him long life. Nor was that all. God gave him continued opportunity and strength to serve Him with that long life, so that in his old age, at eighty-five, he had the greatest victory that he had ever had in all his life. Oh, isn't it glorious for a person to grow old like that? The other day an old preacher came into one of our Workers' Conferences, and he said, "I preached yesterday to my people, and my text was, 'That I might finish my course with joy!' " He said, "I was hedging for myself. I want to finish my course with joy, not to finish it soured and embittered and pessimistic, making everybody miserable about me, but I mean, by God's grace, to finish my course with joy." He said, "I told my country church yesterday I was going in to serve them with more zeal and love than ever before." He will not get old. He will not be a misery to his children and grandchildren. He has the right view-point of life. Caleb had it, and God gave him increased opportunity and strength as a great leader, and then God rewarded him with the great possession that forty-five years before he had seen. And then, with it all, God gave him rest.

O soul! Is Caleb's God yours? Receive Him today to be yours, and follow that God like Caleb followed Him. And if you are here today with all sorts of subterfuges, and evasions, and speculations, and doubtful questions in your life, just be done with them, and just be straightforward and pronounced and true, like Caleb, to God. And your light and day and usefulness in the Christian life will grow brighter and brighter, even until that blissful day when you shall hear the Master say, "It is enough; come home, My friend, to be forever with the Lord."

6

The Temptation of Our Savior

Then was Jesus led up of the Spirit into the wilderness to be tempted of the devil (Matt. 4:1).

The temptation of Jesus was not a visionary one, but it was a real one. He was tempted in all points like as we are, yet without sin. The only difference between His experience and ours is that we yield often to temptation, while He yielded never. It behooved Him to be so that in all respects He would be touched with the feeling of our infirmities; and now no temptation that comes to man is beyond His appreciation and sympathy and help.

It is significant that the temptation of Jesus follows His baptism immediately. During that wonderful baptismal scene the heavens were opened, and God's Spirit descended like a dove and lighted upon Him, and out from the heavens there came a voice which said, "This is My beloved Son, in whom I am well pleased." How swift and surprising are the mutations of human experience! Just after the heavenly proclamation that He is God's Son, immediately comes this sore temptation. Well did a great preacher say, "Do not question the validity of your baptism because it was succeeded by a fierce temptation."That is often true.Triumph is often followed by trial instantly.The hour of exaltation is very often succeeded immediately by the hour of humiliation and trial.The wondrous voice from out the clouds, the heavenly voice, is often succeeded by the voice from beneath, the voice from the pit. Blessed shall it be for us to remember this, and then shall we know that our sonship with God is not dependent upon the rapidly varying moods of our earthly experience.

You will note that this trial of Jesus was not an accident. See the text:"Then was Jesus led up of the Spirit into the wilderness to be tempted of the devil.""Led up to be tempted"—that is not an accident.There is purpose in that. Christ's temptations were not accidental, but they were all included in the great purpose which God had respecting the life and sufferings and death of His Son. "Led up of the Spirit into the wilderness to be tempted of the devil." That is the language. I grant you that there is deep mystery in it, and yet the great truth still abides that God's purpose pours through it all.Take away from life the thought of its education, and you have destroyed the deep meaning of human life."Led up of the Spirit to be tempted of the devil."That is the strange language, and yet the Scriptures show that thought all through their ever unfolding revelations. Not that man is solicited of God to do evil. Never! Never! "Let no man say when he is tempted, I am tempted of God; for God cannot be tempted with evil, neither tempteth He any man." In no instance is man ever tempted of God to do evil, but in many instances, yea, in the instance of the life of every child of God, everyone is subjected to trial, to discipline, to education. Do not the Scriptures clearly show that in the long ago God did tempt Abraham? That is, He tried him; He put him to the test. He subjected him to a process of self-examination and education that more than any other experience would strengthen his character. Understand, then, that trial is an essential part of God's great program for our lives. "Beloved, think it not strange concerning the fiery trial which is to try you, as though some strange thing happened unto you; but rejoice, inasmuch as ye are partakers of Christ's sufferings."

You notice that the Spirit of God here led Jesus "into the wilderness" to have His sore conflict. How often that is the case! Was it not so with Moses for forty long years? If Moses is to formulate the great principles of law and education and religion that are forever to dominate the world's thought and largely shape its life, it is needful that he spend forty years in the wilderness. Likewise also for a season must the wilderness be the home of Elijah. It must needs be true also of John the Baptist, who is to preach repentance as none other ever did preach it, save the Lord. And so of Paul, if he is to be earth's first apostle, he must spend three years in the quiet of Arabia. If Bunyan is to write an allegory that shall be unmatched and forever matchless, he needs the twelve years' imprisonment of Bedford jail. If Milton is to write a poem that has no peer of its kind, he must know the isolation that came to him from blindness and other sore trials. All these wondrous workers must needs be taken into the wilderness, to have a trial, to have a testing time, to go through the discipline of training that the wilderness alone can give them. My brethren, the danger of this age is that people live too much in crowds. No man shall ever come to the highest mark as a thinker and useful worker who lives always in the crowd. We have our magnificent systems of education, and our myriad inventions for the saving of labor and for adding to man's convenience; and then we have the great system of newsgathering, that rains all the news of this planet down at our doors every morning and every evening; and thus, it is to be feared, we are getting away from the race of the world's great thinkers, because we are not led often enough to the wilderness, that there, single-handed and alone, we may think out and fight out some of the deep battles of the inner life.

Let us look at these three temptations that came to Jesus in the wilderness. These three comprehend every possible temptation that ever comes to mankind. First, there was the temptation through the body. After forty days and forty nights of fasting, Jesus is hungry. For days and nights He has been miraculously sustained. Now His human body is thrilled with the sense of hunger. The humanity cries out and gives expression to its pain. Just in the nick of time

the devil appears. Oh, he is an arrant coward. There is not a thing
brave about the devil. He is always sinuous and slimy and cowardly.
He never did a courageous thing in his life. He never came to a
man save at his weak point and at his weak time. Now, when the
humanity of Jesus is put to its sorest test, the shrewd, cowardly imp
of the pit appears and appeals with a temptation to Jesus' hungry
body. What was that temptation? Yielding to it would have meant
what? The yielding to it on the part of Jesus would have meant the
palpable distrust of His Father. Satan said to Him, "Why, you are
hungry. Make bread out of rocks. Turn these stones into biscuit. A
hungry man ought to eat." Jesus could have done it, but to have
yielded to that temptation would have been to show forth absolute
distrust of His Father and utterly discard His guardianship and pro-
tection. And so Jesus hurled back at the tempter the sublime
statement, "It is written, Man shall not live by bread alone, but by
every word that proceedeth out of the mouth of God." Christ here
says that His Father does not have to turn the rocks into bread in
order to sustain the life of His Son. He can preserve life otherwise.
Bread is not the main thing in a man's life. God's Word, proceed-
ing out of His mouth, is far more worthy and helpful than mere
earthly bread. Christ would yield not to the seductive tempter. He
would trust His Father whose providential love would in no wise
fail Him.

That is a piercing temptation, to which all men are subjected,
the temptation that comes to the body. It was by just that that Adam
and Eve were led to fall. The temptation began with an appeal to
the body. With subtle voice the tempter whispered, "The tree is
good for food, and it is pleasant to the eyes, and it is a tree to be desired to make one wise," and by this time Eve was ready to eat of
the fruit, and to give also unto her husband, and even thus was
brought to pass the fall and ruin of the race. The temptation of the
body, its name is legion. There is selfishness, appealing to us on the
one hand with it manifold expressions. There is appetite, pulling and
tugging at the very vitals of our life every day. There is indolence,
that rocks us and soothes us, and continually whispers to us sweet
things about the welfare and comfort of our dear bodies. Appetite

in all its forms unceasingly knocks at the door of our hearts and talks about the necessity of our eating this particular food and doing this particular thing. Well might Paul cry out, "Who shall deliver me from the body of this death?" Very many of the sorest temptations of life come through the body. This one appealed to Jesus through His body, but victoriously He met it, and completely foiled the tempter.

Then the tempter approached our Lord again from an utterly different standpoint. He takes Him up into the holy city, and sets Him on a pinnacle of the temple, and now he makes to Him this remarkable statement: "Cast thyself down, for it is written, He shall give His angels charge concerning thee, and in their hands they shall bear thee up, lest at any time thou dash thy foot against a stone." Do you see how sly it was? This is wonderful for the devil to be quoting Scripture, but he quotes it here, just like he always quotes it. He does not quote it correctly. What he says here does sound like Scripture, but he leaves out the salient point. Here is what he says to the Master: "Cast thyself down; for it is written, He shall give His angels charge concerning thee." Satan fails to quote all the sentence. He left out a few words that were the key to all of it. These were the words left out: "To keep thee in all thy ways." That is to say, God will keep thee in thy rightful ways, in thine appointed ways, in God's providential ways, in the ways marked out by His own infinite wisdom and love. He will keep thee in these ways, but the devil leaves all that qualifying condition out, he omits the vital point of the Scripture. This is a subtle temptation indeed. Do you see its cunning and audacity? It is nothing short of an appeal to Christ to experiment upon the purpose and power of God, and to force meanings into His promises wholly foreign to the intention of His Spirit, and to put God into a situation forbidden both by His Word and nature. Its meaning broadly interpreted is, let man do what he wills, however careless or willful or self-risking it may be. God is pledged to keep him. Criminally sad is this wresting of the divine promises. Just here even many a Christian stumbles to his great shame and harm. He shuts his eyes and presumes upon God. Have you not seen it a hundred times? Men thus trifle with health, with character, with evil influences. They dwell upon their own great strength, they write down strong resolutions, they pray; but they turn from all these into presumptuous sins. God has a plan and limit and purpose and boundary in all that He says and does. He never anywhere says that His child shall be safely upheld if he presumes to cast himself down from the pinnacle of the temple. Only does He promise to keep His children in lawful ways; but they must not presume to dally with danger and say, God will keep me; nor to go forth into sin, saying, grace will abound.

You will also notice that the devil here talks about "angels." "Cast thyself down, and He shall give His angels charge concerning thee." Yes, he talks glibly about "angels." You have heard some men talk with a degree of seeming familiarity with God and His Word, and yet the trend of their lives stamps them as the enemies of the cross of Christ. The devil quoted Scripture and talked about angels and all that, and yet he was the adversary, the seducer, the old dragon of the pit. Quoting Scripture does not mean that a man is in fellowship with God. Talking about angels does not mean that a man has any sort of kinship to them. Jesus repelled this temptation as He did the other, and the devil is hurled into defeat again.

And now Satan comes the third time, and this time he takes Jesus up on an exceeding high mountain, and shows Him all the kingdoms of the world and the glory of them, and then he makes to Jesus this proposal: "If you will fall down and worship me, I will give them all to you." Unparalleled impudence! Unbridled presumption! Not a solitary inch of any of these kingdoms did the devil own, not one has he ever owned, and not one shall he ever own. To be sure, he is here; but he is an intruder here. He is on property that is not his own, and it is the business of the redeemed of God while they abide on the earth to contest every inch of the ground with this personal devil. Nor shall our work be done below till the whole earth be redeemed to God. There is a personal devil operating among men, seeking ever to influence and destroy them, just as literally as there is a personal God seeking to redeem and save. The denial of this proposition is the baldest infidelity.

But suppose the devil had had all those kingdoms of the world that he declaimed about. Suppose they had been his, for argument's sake. Could the Lord have yielded to his proposal? Nay, never; it would have meant instant dethronement of the Almighty. It would have been the instant annihilation of the kingdom of righteousness. What is this proposal here? It is substantially this: The devil says, "Savior, Messiah, Son of God, I have a proposal to make to you. You have three years yet to live. You have just been baptized. You have three years in which to preach and suffer, and to be scourged, and to be wounded in heart, both by your enemies and friends, and at the end to die on the shameful tree of the cross. You have all that ahead of you. Suppose you and I go into partnership. You bow down and say just one prayer to me, and I will make you a title deed to all of this business. Let us go into partnership. Let us have an amalgamation of heaven and hell. Let us have a compromise of the two great establishments upon mutual terms, and then the lion and the lamb will lie down side by side, and the devil and God will be twin brothers, and there will be no conflict at all. That means for you, O Jesus, no humiliation, no weariness, nor pain, nor conflict with all the complexities and difficulties of your plan of salvation. And it also means for you, O Jesus, no betrayal, no dark Gethsemane, no Calvary and no death. Take a nearer route to rulership. Just make one concession to Satan, and he will vacate the field, and you shall have it all your own way." That is Satan's distinct proposal in that awful hour.

Shall the Lord just pander one moment to this proposal from the pit? Is there anywhere any possible amalgamation of the principles of righteousness with the principles of unrighteousness? Nay, never; it cannot be. If Jesus had that day bowed before Satan and said: "I will say one prayer unto thee, O Satan, for just one minute," the kingdom of righteousness would have been forever annihilated that same minute. That momentary compromise would have meant defeat eternal to the kingdom of God.

There is a vast field of thought, my brethren, here in this last point. There is not to be a scintilla of compromise between the kingdom of evil and the kingdom of righteousness. Any pandering to any of the principles of the kingdom of evil is but a yielding to this subtle seduction and temptation of the devil, when he asked Christ on the mountain to give him one moment's concession and worship. That moment would have meant eternal treason to truth, to righteousness, and to God.

Deep and broad is the lesson suggested by this third temptation. There is not one inch of room for pretense or double-dealing in the kingdom of God.

Every questionable method in Christ's church, of any shape, form, or fashion is but the pandering to the kingdom of evil and the yielding to this third temptation that came to Christ. 'Tis the same old suggestion that so oft we hear: "Let us do evil that good may come." Every such policy is the palpable and fundamental violation and subversion of every principle inculcated by God's Word. I do not hesitate to say this morning that if Christ's praying one prayer unto Satan that day would have won all the world, He could not have made such concession. A salvation so effected would have been no salvation at all. The Lord, He is God, and to Him alone shall be given homage and worship. For Jesus to have made one concession would have been the utter annihilation of His own righteous character, and His own rightful authority over the children of men. You must not do evil that good may come. If, by the doing of some present evil, you think you can see good out there in the distance, you are not to do it. You are not allowed to do evil whatever the allurement or harvest promised. That is identically what Satan here proposes: "O Christ, do a little evil, and I will get off the ground! Say one prayer to me, and I will vacate the whole territory." But the Lord held out in the conflict steadily against Satan, and repelled him a third time with the wondrous sentences of His Father's Word. Somebody has suggestively said that "of all the essences that the devil likes, he best likes acquiescence." "Resist the devil, and he will flee from you." And the supreme weapon for such resistance is that same conquering one used by Christ: "It is written." In all your conflicts with temptation, O Christian, take "the sword of the Spirit which is the Word of God."

Did you ever notice where the Lord got all these quotations? He got them from the book of Deuteronomy. I haven't a doubt that our Lord knew that many centuries later certain clever little men would be trying to destroy this book of Deuteronomy. This is the book they are specially after now. The divine Son of God, looking down through the ages, saw the coming conflict, and He got these quotations out of the book that He knew would be so vehemently attacked.

There is this other suggestion in such quotation—the overwhelming argument for the verbal inspiration of God's Word. Not simply the inspiration of ideas, not simply the inspiration of thoughts, but the inspiration of the very words of God's Book. That is an intangible, mazy, far-off, unapproachable, indefinable, inexplicable species of inspiration that leaves out the plenary, verbal inspiration of the Holy Scriptures. Jesus here forever gives this book His endorsement.

But now, after these three conflicts with the tempter, what becomes of the Savior? The devil is completely routed; but what of the Savior? Here is the answer: "Behold, angels came and ministered unto Him." All during that dreadful conflict, lingering near by, the angels of God watched the awful struggle, as the Son of God did meet in the open field the dark fiend of the pit, and contest with him every inch of the ground. And now, when the devil is baffled, defeated and driven away, the "angels came and ministered unto Jesus." Thus it is evermore. When Jesus prayed in Gethsemane that last awful night, before He took up the march to the cross, saying, "Nevertheless, not My will, but Thine be done," "an angel appeared unto Him from heaven, strengthening Him." An angel came when Elijah was yonder, speeding away from the land of his enemies, who sought to destroy him. He rests yonder in the mountains, hungry, and weary, and alone. An angel came and brought food unto him. The angels, doubtless, are spectators in all our conflicts with the temptations of life. "The angel of the Lord encampeth round about them that fear Him, and delivereth them."

What is the outstanding lesson today for us in all this story of God's temptation? The lesson is for us to hold right on to the right, ever repelling the tempter with this sure weapon which our Lord did use—"It is written." Oh, be not misled and overcome by the old fiend of the pit. Evermore stand on the sure Word of God, and here shall you find rest and victory for your souls.

There are two plans whereby men may resist temptation. The one has been called "The plan of resistance"; the other "The plan of counter-attraction." Both are illustrated from stories in Greek mythology. The one finds illustration in the story of the Greeks who must sail by the Island of the Sirens, as they returned from Troy. Bewitching strains of music came to the Greeks as they neared the island, so that they were seized with the desire to throw themselves into the sea and swim to the sirens. But this would have meant their certain and speedy death, and for this alone the treacherous sirens sang their enchanting songs. Then the leader made the Greeks to fill their ears with wax, and had himself bound thoroughly to the boat so that when they passed the shore where the sirens dwelled, and they should begin their strains of entrancing music, the men with stopped ears could not hear, and the leader, though he should wish to go, would be bound hand and foot so that he could not; and thus they could make the journey in safety. This is the method of resistance, but that method is not the best. The other story illustrated the other method, the method of counter-attraction. It is the story of the Argonauts, who sailed with Jason in search of the golden fleece, and they also had to round that same southern shore of Italy, where sang the sirens. They took on board with them Orpheus whose music entranced the very beasts of the forests, and made even the trees to wave before him in homage. And now as they come where the sirens dwell, and as the sirens begin to play the soft music, Orpheus strikes the wondrous notes of his lyre, so that all the air vibrates with the sweet melodies, and all the sailors on the boat laugh to scorn the sirens, and the voyagers round the shore in safety. That is the method whereby you and I are to overcome temptation in the experiences of our earthly life. This alone is the sure way of triumph. "This I say, then, Walk in the spirit, and ye shall not fulfill the lusts of the flesh." "Ye shall know the truth, and the truth shall make you free." "If the Son shall make you free, you shall be free, indeed."

O my wearied, battling, tempted friends, whether saved or lost, freely and fully admit Jesus into your heart and life, and then shall you overcome. And know that if left to your own poor strength, you shall surely go down before temptation's power. Will you not heed His precious call today? It is this: "Behold, I stand at the door and knock; if any man hear My voice, and open the door, I will come to him, and will sup with him, and he with Me." "And whosoever will, let him take the water of life freely." Come to Him now. Cast yourself utterly and forever upon Him, and you shall find rest for your soul.

7

Intercessory Prayer

Moreover as for me, God forbid that I should sin against the Lord in ceasing to pray for you (1 Sam. 12:23).

he text is one of the concluding statements of the address of the prophet Samuel to his people. I read you the chapter a moment ago, that you might see the setting of the text. Samuel was God's prophet, and spoke to the people the things that God would have them know, that knowing they might obey. But after a while they became impatient under his counsel and leadership, and clamored for a king, and so persistently clamored, that Saul was anointed king over them. And then the prophet reminded them of his advanced age, of his gray hairs, of his long life of service for them; and in his last words to them, reminded them that sin, whenever and by whomsoever committed, would be punished by the Almighty; and if they expected God's mercy and blessings, sin must be put away from them, and obedience to the commandments of God must characterize all their ways. In his address there was brought home to the people a realization of the gravity of their sin, that they had even gone to the desperate length of discarding God's prophet and clamoring for a selfish, ambitious king to be their leader. And so they cried unto the prophet in their distress and under the sense of their terrible situation, that he would pray God not to leave them to their wicked devices, nor to allow the calamity to overtake them that even then was impending. His noble answer was this "Moreover as for me, God forbid that I should sin against the Lord in ceasing to pray for you."

It is one of the sublimest utterances that ever fell from any man's lips, especially when you take into consideration the circumstances of such utterance. The old man has lived unselfishly for his people. He has wrought with all possible devotion and self-abnegation through a long life for his people. Not for himself has he wrought, but for them, for their welfare, for their happiness, for the great causes and principles that made for their profit, both for the present and for the future. Now, at the close of his notable life, they discard him and discredit him. And then later they turn to him in their desperation and extremity, by reason of their sins, and ask him to pray for them, and he answers: "As for me, God forbid that I should sin against the Lord in ceasing to pray for you." It is a marvelous utterance.

The text suggests the measureless importance of intercessory prayer. Upon that theme I would speak this morning: The importance of intercessory prayer. It goes without any argument that very few, if any of us, realize properly the far-reaching moment of intercessory prayer in carrying on the cause of God in this world. Our text suggests, first of all, our responsibility to God for our praying. When they appeal to Samuel not to cease to pray for them, the prophet answered, "I could not so sin against God as to cease to pray for you." Our praying, then, has a relation of personal responsibility in the sight of God. Man is responsible for every opportunity with which his life is in any way invested. All of life's talents, its privileges, its opportunities, are gifts from the Almighty to us, and unto Him we are responsible for the use or the abuse of them all. Man is responsible for the abuse made of his education, for the education that he does have, for the education that he can have. For the best possible development of the resources of mind and heart and life every man is responsible. Man is likewise responsible for his influence. If he could bring to pass certain great causes for the welfare of men and the glory of his Maker, by the use of his influence, then he shall justly be held accountable in the sight of the Almighty for such use or abuse of influence. Man is responsible for the use or abuse of his money, and he unto whom the Lord gives the power to get wealth shall as certainly be held responsible for the use or abuse of that talent as any man in the world entrusted with any other gift.

Now, prayer is one of the supreme opportunities that God has vouchsafed unto men for the forwarding of His kingdom among men. Prayer is a force. Paul talks about "helping together by prayer." And for using or abusing such opportunity, God will hold every one of us accountable. Prayer has then, first of all, a direct reference to God; and when we look upon it like that, there comes home to us the painful discovery of how much we have doubtless lost by the neglect of this opportunity that God has offered us. We talk about latent powers. We talk about the latent power of steam, that wrapped up, undisclosed, hidden power, of which the world for so long a time did not have any just conception at all, not even when its power began first to be discovered and used. We talk about the latent power of electricity, that now speaks messages around the world in one or two moments. How little we knew about that latent power until just a few years ago. But the most marvelous latent power in the world is the latent power of prayer. Do you doubt that things all about us would be different if we had prayed as we ought? Do you doubt that conditions in Church and in State would be marvelously changed from what they now are if the sons of men had called upon God as they ought?

There are manifest reasons why men do not realize the power of intercessory prayer. A number of them will occur to us as we think upon the subject. Men do not realize the responsibility and moment of intercessory prayer, because they do not stop to think that prayer is more than a privilege. Prayer is a God-enjoined duty. It is not optional with us whether or not we shall pray for men. It is a direct command from the Almighty for us to pray for men, for all men, without leaving one out in all the world. That is a God-enjoined duty, as plainly indicated in His Scriptures as is any other truth there indicated. We have too much looked upon this matter of praying as a matter of privilege. To be sure, it is a glorious privilege, an exalted privilege, an incomparable privilege, this privilege of preferring our requests before God. Oh! If we had to come home to us the awful realization that God would not hear us, no matter how we called upon Him, it would paralyze us and overwhelm us. Blessed and exalted above all words is the privilege of prayer!

But prayer is a great deal more than a privilege. Prayer is a God-given duty, and no man is excused from it, no matter what his belief, or character, or condition in life. God asks all men to pray, to prefer their requests before Him, to come unto Him continually, and tell Him out of their hearts, their hopes and fears and needs and desires. We have too much looked upon it simply as a privilege to be used or not, according to our own wish.

And, again, we have not realized as we ought the need and the danger of men all about us, for whom we are to pray. Oh, if we could have the curtains that separate us from eternity lifted, so that we might have just one glance at the danger of men all about us, the one thing we would do would be to betake ourselves at once to our rooms, and fall down there upon our faces before the Almighty, and entreat His mercy and favor and gracious hand of deliverance in their behalf.

Still again, we do not realize this matter as we ought, because the answer to our prayers is so often delayed. Time and time again different ones of you have come to me and said, "I have asked—God witnesseth the truth of what I say—I have asked for Him to do this or that or the other thing for me, and yet no answer has come." "Hope deferred maketh the heart sick," and after a while the anxious mother droops in her prayers, wanes in her expectations, goes down under the withering paralysis of distrust of God, and to a large degree ceases to pray. And so it goes with the devoted, clinging, patient, trustful, Christian wife, as she beseeches God for the strong man by her side, that he may be saved. Because the answer is often long delayed, we cease to pray as we ought, leaving the whole matter, in some stoical, unbelieving way, to the arbitrament of the Almighty, in whom is infinite wisdom and from whom must come every needed blessing.

But now for whom is intercessory prayer to be offered? Paul, in his first letter to Timothy, leaves us without any sort of doubt about the persons for whom prayer is to be offered. You read that epistle and you will see that he thus enjoins prayer: "I exhort, therefore, that, first of all, supplications, prayers, intercessions and giving of thanks be made for all men; for kings, and for all that are in authority"—that is, "in eminent place," as the marginal reading gives it, and the Revised Version, "all that are in high place." Why? "That we may lead a quiet and peaceable life in all godliness and honesty." Note his exhortation well: "I exhort that supplications, prayers, and intercessions be made for all men." That is his injunction as to our prayers. Look at it a moment. He enjoins that we shall pray for all who are in authority, who are in an eminent place. Look at the different classes that would come under that head. There might be mentioned, first of all, the rulers of state, men in positions of government, men who rule, men who make and execute laws. For these the mighty apostle enjoins that there shall be prayer, unceasing, intercessory prayer. And it will readily occur to us that such praying is to be offered in behalf of men in authority, without regard to their political principles and preferment. God's people are to pray for all who are in authority, however much they may differ from them in politics or in the principles to which these men subscribe. We owe it as a duty unto the Almighty to pray unceasingly for all such men in positions of state about us. And do you have the shadow of doubt that law would be better in its construction and better in its enforcement, if daily the sons and daughters of the Almighty made intercessions for the right construction and enforcement of law by those who sit in eminent position? Beyond a doubt, every man of us must plead guilty to the charge that we do not pray enough for men in authority, for men who make laws, and our other men who seek to execute the laws, for men in chief positions, where men gather around them and take their cue of life largely from these men who are invested with leadership. Oh, the responsibility of such a public man! His position is a position attracting the attention of uncounted hosts of men; and if he be bad, and if he be careless of influence, and if he disregard his relations to God, and if he be without concern for the great principles of righteousness and truth, what a hurtful mark he will leave in the land in which he lives. God's men and women are enjoined in Holy Scripture, directly and indirectly, to offer intercessory prayer for men in public position. And, I repeat, there is not the shadow of a doubt that law would be better constructed and better enforced if the lawmakers and executives had the unceasing prayers of the people in their behalf. It is not simply a question of privilege for us, O brethren; it is a question of duty, enjoined directly and specifically upon us by the Almighty Himself.

The reasons for this are manifest. Office is deceptive. Position is always a thing of great danger. Office is a thing full many a time so deceptive as utterly to mislead men. Men after a while in position are tempted to reach the place that Nebuchadnezzar reached, when he said, "Is not this great Babylon which I have builded?" "Which I have builded." The Almighty was utterly left out. And so position is ever a thing deceptive; and for that reason men in public station, either in Church or State, need the unceasing intercessions of the people of God. And I repeat that the question of politics hasn't anything in the world to do with our duty. Christ's church knows nothing of political lines in it. It was uttered some time ago, very foolishly, by a minister who should know better, that he would not be the pastor of a church if every man in it did not vote a certain way. The statement was extremely foolish and improper. No such lines as that are to be drawn in the church of Jesus Christ. Without any regard to a man's political affiliations, or principles, or platform, God's people are enjoined to offer prayer, fervently and unceasingly, that men in authority may be guided aright, that through such guidance the people may lead quiet and peaceable lives in all godliness and honesty.

Then there are others besides civil officers that are in eminent place. Oh! in what eminent positions are the ministers of the Lord Jesus Christ, and how great their need of the constant intercessions of the people of God! Brethren, if the apostle Paul would write like this: "I beseech you, pray for me," how much more the ordinary preacher needs to send forth that cry to the people. Paul said, "I beseech you, brethren, for the Lord Jesus Christ's sake, and for the love of the Spirit, that ye strive together with me in your prayers to God for me." If earth's greatest preacher would make such a plea as that, how much more the humble, ordinary, insignificant preacher needs to throw himself at the feet of the people, begging such intercessions from them in his behalf!

Now, why is it so? The temptations of Christ's preacher are manifold and grave. He is tempted all along to professionalism; and when Christ's preacher preaches merely to preach, then his usefulness is at an end. When Christ's preacher fails to preach with the great throbbing passion and purpose that brought the Son of God to the earth, that He might live and die to make expiatory atonement for the sins of a lost world, his usefulness as a minister of Jesus Christ is already at an end. He is tempted to professionalism all along, and professionalism in the ministry means death to the preaching of the gospel. He is tempted to vanity by the applause of the world. Whenever Christ's minister is lifted up with pride by the applause of men, already that man's deterioration and decline have begun, and if he follows on in that inexcusable way, he shall sink to uselessness in the kingdom of God.

The reasons are many, dear brethren, why God's ministers are to be constantly upborne by the people in their intercessions. A praying church makes a successful preacher. You may take any humble little preacher, and let him be buttressed about by a church, that day in and day out beseeches God to make him valiant and skillful and strong in the Lord and in the power of His might, and he will be a mighty preacher. I care not who he is. The world is filled with examples demonstrating that selfsame truth. They tell us that before Mr. Spurgeon preached, every Sunday morning and evening, a half hour was spent by his large body of church officers praying just for the blessing of God upon the preacher and the people for that service. He might never preach again, and the people might never come back again, or some man who, in the providence of God, had come to that service might never come back again. And therefore they waited at the throne of grace, praying that the breath of the Almighty might be upon the preacher's message, that men might be turned to the Lord and be saved. And out from such holy atmosphere the mighty preacher came every time he stood up in his vast tabernacle to preach the word of grace to the gathered thousands. A praying church makes a mighty preacher.

And you may take any church where they do not pray for the preacher, and the preacher there, no matter who he is, gets on poorly. There is an atmosphere in the kingdom of God, and that atmosphere is as real as is the atmosphere in this physical world about us; and the atmosphere in which the preacher of God preaches is of untold moment in the matter of his preaching and usefulness for the lost world unto whom he is sent to preach. When John Livingstone stood up and preached at Shotts, in the days past, a great many people were amazed at his preaching, for under one sermon on one occasion five hundred souls publicly acknowledged Jesus Christ as their personal Savior. When they looked into the matter, they found that the night before, several hundred had prayed all night that the next morning, God's Spirit might so rest upon the preacher, that a backslidden church and community might find out again that God had power upon earth to save men.

The same story is substantially true of Jonathan Edwards. When that wonderful revival came to Yale University, in a past generation, people seemed unable to account for such remarkable scenes in that nobly historic old university. When they looked into the matter, it was found that for weeks and weeks every ministerial student in that school, along with a number of other Christian young men, had risen up before daylight, every morning, and had gone to a certain room in the building, and had poured out their hearts to God, that old Yale might be shaken with a heaven-sent revival, and it came. Can you doubt that it came because of this intercessory prayer?

I have been rereading recently the story of Charles G. Finney, one of the most eminent and successful ministers that America has ever produced. Mr. Finney's revival meetings are yet matters of note throughout all the theological world. He gives an account of his notable campaigns for religion in the state of New York: Great meetings were held, when hundreds and thousands of strong men accepted the Savior, in Utica, and in Binghamton, and in Syracuse, and in Rochester, mighty meetings, you remember, if you have read the story, when hundreds and thousands of men, among them congressmen and judges and lawyers and eminent men in every station, came to Jesus Christ. Mr. Finney in writing about it afterwards tells us that there was a thing going on all the time that he did not know anything about. It was this: There was a plain man in that state who was a minister, but who preached with exceeding poverty of speech and power so far as his public speech was concerned. But he prayed; and when Mr. Finney came to that state, this plain man, Abel Clary, betook himself to prayer, shut himself up in his study and gave himself for weeks, and even for months, unceasingly to prayer, and in his journal, the simple diary that Clary kept, were found long afterwards such entries as these: "I have been strangely moved today to pray for the salvation of Utica, and I have prayed for a week for Utica." And then again, "I have been strangely moved today to pray for the salvation of Rochester, and I have prayed for Rochester for a week." Nobody knew anything about it but the one man, but after he was dead, Mr. Finney saw the simple diary, and at the very times when Mr. Finney was preaching the gospel publicly with such unexampled power in these several New York cities, this plain man was on bended knee, interceding with God to save those same cities. Do you doubt that there was a vital connection between that man's humble praying and the marvelous results that attended Mr. Finney's preaching? Such illustrations might be multiplied indefinitely.

Prayer is to be offered for all men. How much the teachers need prayer, both the secular and the religious teachers. Do you parents pray for the men and the women who teach your boys and girls in the public schools? If you are neglecting that you are neglecting one of the most delicately and eternally responsible matters in the world. Do you parents pray for the men and the women that teach your children in the Sunday school classes? They are hammering upon these plastic hearts, and as they hammer, so shall be character and destiny to an awful degree with such children, for time and eternity. Prayer unceasing is to be offered for them all.

But Paul sums it all up by asking that prayer be made for ALL men. You will notice that by example and precept there were several classes for whom Jesus urges us to pray. He teaches us to pray for the sick. That is the reason we had prayer this morning, and why we have prayers at every prayer-meeting, for our beloved members who are sick. A man brought to Jesus his afflicted boy and said to Him, "I want your help." And Jesus healed him. Then the disciples took Jesus aside and said, "We tried to heal him, and why could not we do it?" And He said, "This kind can come forth by nothing but by prayer." And then again the apostle James teaches us that God is well pleased with our prayer when we present the sick unto Him. Of course, it must be ever understood when we present our loved ones in their distress unto God that we are to submit to the will of God, whatever that may be.

Then there was this other class for which Jesus prayed, and for which we are to pray, and that was the children. You remember the account given in the nineteenth chapter of Matthew, where the mothers brought their children unto Jesus that He might lay His hands upon them and pray. Wouldn't you have rejoiced to have heard one of those prayers Jesus made for that little girl or that little boy that the mother brought to Him? Do you suppose He said, "Father, make this child to be rich in this world's goods"? Do you suppose He said, "Father, let this child be heavenly minded; let this child love Jesus Christ; let this child give its life to the noblest and the sublimest things." Don't you know in your soul that He prayed like that? Surely, surely, we are to pray for our children. As the child goes, so shall go the world, and therefore prayer unceasing is to be made for these dear young lives, unable yet to apprehend the deep responsibilities of human life.

Again, Jesus teaches us that we are to pray for all His people everywhere; not merely for a particular church, not merely for a particular denomination, but we are to pray for the true Israel of God everywhere, in all this earth. "Pray one for another" is the voice of Jesus to His people in every age and in every land.

And, still again, He teaches us that there is another class to pray for, and I want you to see it as a positive command: "Pray for them which despitefully use you and persecute you." There is His specific, direct command. That is a command that may not be avoided, that may not be disputed, that may not be disregarded. We are to pray for the men who despitefully use us and persecute us. And right there is the heroic place in Christianity. An unsaved man cannot do it. An unsaved man cannot from his heart crave the favor of God upon his persecuting enemies. God's man can do it, by the grace of God. And not only can he, but he is enjoined by the Almighty to do that specific thing. O brethren, will we never learn that the gospel of hate is the gospel of destruction? Will we never learn that for a man to hate is for him to pursue a pathway of folly, the end of which is filled with the most lamentable consequences? Will we never learn that hate incapacitates a man for the noblest and truest living? Will we never learn that to hate fills the heart with rancorous, unholy impulses, which unfit us to an awful degree for the solemn work of human life? "Pray for them which despitefully use you and persecute you." I hope you know the sweetness of that same experience. I hope you know what it is when you have been maltreated by someone to go alone with God, and to commend that one to His mercy, and to beseech the Almighty that good and not evil may come upon the head of that one. If you have learned that, you have learned one of the deepest, sweetest, holiest experiences that the human heart can ever know.

I am speaking too long upon this vital theme, and I must close. We talk a great deal about "unanswered prayers." Let us then rather think about our unoffered prayers. Your boy might have been saved if you had prayed as you ought. I declare it upon the authority of God's book. Your husband might have been saved if you had prayed as you ought, and lived rightly along with the praying. I declare it upon the authority of that same book. Some man for whose soul you yearn might long ago have stood up in the presence of the people of God, saying, "Your God is mine, your hope mine," if you and I and all of us had prayed for that man as we ought. One of the deepest regrets of my life, I confess it to you today, is that I have prayed so little for lost sinners, compared with what I ought to have prayed. O my people, our children, our loved ones, to an awful degree are dependent upon our prayers. And there are lost men, rulers of state, businessmen, laborers and capitalists, the rich and the poor, the old and the young, all about us; God forbid that we should so sin against the Lord as to cease praying for them! Let us pray for them here and now with all our hearts! The Lord help us and hear us!

8

The Growth of Faith

And there was a certain nobleman, whose son was sick at
Capernaum (John 4:46).

*A*re there those here tonight who wish to be
Christians? Doesn't that dear boy over there
wish to be a Christian, and that older one,
turning into young manhood, and the young man himself there,
and that young woman—don't you wish to be Christians? Then,
listen, will you not, to the simple exposition of the Scripture that
has just been read?

It is good for us to see the matter illustrated of how one
comes to Christ and secures His blessing. It is good to note how
faith is illustrated, as it is again and again in the Scriptures. It is illustrated here in the case of this nobleman, who came to Jesus with
a great burden, and made to Him a great request, and received from
Him a great blessing. Let us look back a moment to the circumstances that led up to this nobleman's visit and appeal to Jesus.

The nobleman was in trouble. He was a nobleman, mark you,
of some position and prominence; and yet that did not save him
from knowing what it was to be in trouble. That old Spanish

proverb is true which says, "There is no home without its hush." The proverb itself carries with it its own plain meaning. "There is no home without its hush." Every home, however high it may be, and prominent and wealthy, or if it be low and humble and obscure, every home has about it something that, sooner or later, brings to it a hush. It is so with every home represented here tonight. Man is prone to have trouble in this world, and if we have missed it thus far, the day comes on apace when our hearts shall be wrung to their depths, perhaps, with some great sorrow. Let us not imagine that there is any class, or any family, that will escape trouble sooner or later. It will, sooner or later, find its way into the palace or castle, as well as the hovel of the very poor. "Man is born unto trouble, as the sparks fly upward."

This nobleman's trouble was about his child. His child was now sick, near to the point of death, and the man's heart was stirred with grievous concern for his child. This is always a most tender sight, to see a parent's watchfulness for his child, to see a parent's concern for his child, a parent's love for his child. Out of the Old Testament Scriptures, is there anything more heart-wringing than David's lament for his son Absalom, that poor, wretched fellow, who was so little of a man, who was so much of a scapegrace—that son who brought such distress upon his father? Yet when the worst came, and the lad's life was ended, the old man with unutterable grief wrung his hands and cried: "O my son Absalom, my son, my son Absalom! Would God I had died for thee, O Absalom, my son, my son!" It is the picture of a true parent's love for his child, however wicked and worthless the child. Oh, if this parental anxiety could always be carried deeper than mere material things! If parents who would die for their children, who would take out of their mouths the last bite of food to give to their children, if these parents would just go deeper than that, and look after their children in their supreme needs, how blessed it would be. If parents would put themselves out for the spiritual welfare of their children, so directing their lives, so ordering their own examples as parents! If parents would do that, then how many the heartaches from which they would be delivered, and how many the disasters they would miss! When children in a home are worldly and careless and godless, back of it all there is a fearful cause.

It is good when trouble leads a man to God instead of away from God. It will always do one of these two things. The nobleman's trouble brought him to God. Friend, are you in trouble? Come with it to God. In this man's coming to Christ there is an illustration of the growth of faith from the lowest to the highest degree. Note the several degrees of faith.

First of all, this man sought Jesus' help. That is the very first step in one's coming to Christ. I mean, of course, from the human side. This man sought Jesus' help. He was yonder, a day's journey away from where Jesus was, and when he heard that Jesus had come back to a certain familiar locality, the man hastened from his house and from his sick child, and with all speed came a day's journey to lay before Jesus, face to face, the case of his boy. He sought Jesus. That is the first great step, then, in coming to Jesus. "If thou seek Him, He will be found of thee." "Seek ye the Lord while He may be found." "In the day that thou seekest Me with thy whole heart, I will be found of thee." "They that seek Me early shall find Me." "Ye shall seek Me and find Me, when ye shall search for Me with all your heart." So the very first step in our coming to Christ for salvation is that we seek Him—that we earnestly put ourselves into the great business of finding Him. This man sought Jesus. He used the means to come into contact with Him. He came to where Jesus was. He poured out his heart to Jesus, which is but another name for praying; for when we talk to Jesus, and tell Him of our needs and of our wishes, then it is that we are praying.

This man did all that, but there was a weakness in it. What was it? Jesus saw the weakness and exposed it to the man. The man said, "Sir, come down ere my child die." That was the weakness. The man was telling Jesus how He must do, in order for the child to live. "Come down," he said. "Come and go with me; go where you can see the boy, where you can talk to him, where he can talk to you; come down ere my child die." Do you not see the fundamental mistake in that man's appeal? See what Jesus said to him: "Nobleman, except ye see signs and wonders, ye will not believe." That is to say, "Aren't you demanding signs and wonders before you will put the boy's case into My hands at all?" Just here is the vital mistake made by the seeker after God. As long as the soul dictates to Jesus how He shall bless, it shall not get His blessing. As long as the soul states terms to Jesus, it shall have no favor of Him, no forgiving love. So Jesus put this man to the test, and said in effect: "Aren't you demanding that I shall work signs, that I shall do wonders for you, before you will commit your boy to Me at all?" The man saw the vital point, and relinquished his boy without reservation or dictation into Jesus' hands.

O sinner, listen to this simple statement: Since Jesus does the saving, does all of it, won't you let Him save you His way? You will never be saved any other way. You will never be saved at all, be sure of it, until you just let Jesus save you His own way. Now tonight He would save you. He wishes to save you now. There is no doubt about that. Today is the accepted time always with Him, and never tomorrow. Now, tonight, in this place, there are some who are not saved. Do you wish to be? Won't you now say, "Lord, Jesus, I will not say that Thou must bless me this way or that way, or some other way. I simply ask that Thou wilt bless in Thine own divine way, and I do make absolute surrender of my case now and forever to Thee." Won't you thus yield yourselves to Christ? If you will, you shall be saved here tonight. O Spirit of God, wilt Thou not draw these lost ones thus to trust themselves to Christ?

And now here appears the second degree or manifestation of the nobleman's faith. What was it? When the nobleman relinquished the boy into Jesus' hands, Jesus said to him: "Go thy way; thy son liveth." And the Scriptures go further and say: "And the man believed the word that Jesus had spoken unto him, and he went on his way." Right there is the seeking sinner saved. "The man believed the word that Jesus had spoken unto him." The man really took Jesus at His word. Right there the seeking sinner is saved. The sinner may weep; the sinner may pray; the sinner may be filled with great grief; the sinner's heart may be sorely wrenched and disturbed; the sinner may be cast down and filled with gloom unutterable, and yet go down, and deeper down and be forever lost, unless he takes Jesus at His word, and closes in with Him. When Jesus says, "Him that cometh to Me, I will in no wise cast out," the seeking sinner is to answer back and say, "Lord, I will come; I will surrender to Thee; I will take Thee to be my Savior; though I do not understand it, yet it is enough for me that Thou dost invite me. Gladly therefore do I yield; I surrender forever to Thee. I take Thee at Thy word; living or dying, I give my all to Thee." Right there the sinner is saved.

O lost one, now listening so earnestly to what I am saying, if Jesus were here tonight, and He should say, "Will you trust your soul to Me? If you will, I will save you." What would be your answer? He will not force you. He will not bind you hand and foot and tie you and drag you in. Christ does not save that way. Christ sends His Word and His Spirit to show you your need, to show you your duty, to show you your danger, to convince your mind and awaken your heart. He thus sets before you life and death. He says, "The soul that will surrender utterly to Jesus shall have life." He also says, "The soul that keeps away from Jesus, and refuses to rely upon Jesus, must go down, forever down, unto spiritual death." Now when the soul just closes in with Christ, and says, "I will take Him at His word," such soul is saved. His word states: "Commit thy way unto the Lord; trust also in Him, and He shall bring it to pass." "Then I will commit my way to Thee, just as Thou hast said. I close in with Thee, Lord Jesus, just as Thou hast bidden me do, receiving Thee to be my Savior." Whenever the soul does that, Christ saves such soul.

Do you see the nobleman going yonder? He is singing. Ten minutes ago his face was covered with the lines of anxious sorrow. Now he is singing. Listen how he sings, how cheerily he sings. Let us stop him and talk with him: "Nobleman, why that joyous singing?" "My boy is better." "When did you hear from him?" "Yesterday; I left home yesterday." "How was he when you left?" "He was at the point of death." "And is that the last time you have heard?" "Yes, yes, it is the last time I have heard." "Ten minutes ago, Mr. Nobleman, your face was covered with distress and sorrow. Now it is all gone. Why this change?" "Because I put my boy's case into the hands of Jesus, and He said that He would heal him, and

I have taken Him at His word." "Is that all, Nobleman?" "That is all." "Do you mean to say that what He said is the occasion for your joy?" "That is just it." "Do you mean to say that the reason why you are now happy is what Jesus said to you?" "Yes, I mean that; He has said that my boy is to live and I take Him at His word; He has said it, and I am going back rejoicing; He has said it, and I expect to find it just like He said it; He has said it, and He will keep His word; that is the reason for all my joy." Right there the soul is saved. O sinner, close in with Jesus, take Him now at His word.

For the soul just to take Jesus at His word is the simplest thing in the world, if only the soul may see it. I said to a young man in the congregation last night, who tarried after the service, and who was deeply distressed about his soul: "What would you do if Jesus Christ stood here by your side, in person, so that you could see Him, and touch Him and talk to Him face to face? And if He made to you the distinct proposal: 'Young man, with all your sins, and fears, and doubts, and difficulties, mentally, morally and of every other character, if with them all you will make the surrender of yourself utterly and forever to Me, I will save and keep you,' what would be your answer?" In the twinkling of an eye he said, "Why, I would do it." Then I sought to show him from the Word of God that the way of life is that simple. God comes to the sinner and says, "Sinner, give Me your heart." The sinner answers, "It is a bad heart." "Yes, I will make it good." "It is a sinful heart, Lord." "Yes, that is the reason I call for you; it needs to be saved; it needs to be made anew." "Well, Lord, I cannot understand it." "I did not say that; I said, trust it to Me." "Well, Lord, I have this serious trouble and that." And He answers, "Come along with all your troubles, and I will manage every one of them for you; I will save you unto the uttermost; I know all about your every difficulty, and every sin and every fear; I came on purpose to save sinners. Will you trust Me, that I may save you? If ever you are saved, I must save you." The soul that sincerely answers, "Lord, I close in with Thee, receiving Thee to be mine and giving myself to be Thine forever," right there such soul is saved.

May I take a leaf out of my own little life, as I sought the Savior? I went for years seeking the Savior. I do not believe there was a day in all those years, from my boyhood up to young manhood, I do not believe there was a day that I was not more or less seeking the Savior. But what misconceptions I had about the way to be saved! I believe now, as I study the Scriptures, and study Christian experience, and study my own experience, it seems to me now that if any man at any time during those several years had come to me and had shown me just this: "If you are ready here and right now to give yourself, your all, to Jesus Christ to be His forever, receiving Him to be yours," it seems to me now that if any man had put it that way to me, I would have decided for Christ in one moment. I believe it would have been closed with me, determined by me in a moment. This matter of the soul's salvation is a matter of direct dealing with the personal Christ. He says: "What wilt thou that I should do unto thee?"

Now, what is Christ's Word? Here is one of His sayings: "Him that cometh to Me I will in no wise cast out." That includes you, my child. "Him that cometh to Me I will in no wise cast out." That includes you, my young man. Why, do you think this good and all-merciful Savior would push you away tonight if you said from your heart: "Lord, I will give up to Thee." Do you think He would reject you? Why, the one great thing that He is concerned about is that sinners may come to Him. He calls men to preach, that they may tell of His mercy to those who need to be saved. He has His churches in the world for the same great purpose. He sends His Spirit to impress the lost, and to move upon Christian hearts to pray for the lost. All these gracious agencies are to bring you to say "yes" to Jesus, to persuade you to give up to Jesus, just to surrender yourself forever to Jesus. Won't you do it? He receives you, and saves you, with His own great salvation. Just take Him at His word. You never can save yourself, never, forever. If you went around this world on your knees, leaving blood prints every time you moved, that would not save you. Christ must save, and Christ alone.

> In my hand no price I bring,
> Simply to Thy cross I cling.

You are just to receive Christ, to save you in His own way. Are you ready thus to receive Him tonight? Will you now thus receive

Him? If so, you will go home tonight one of the Lord's believing children. Will you do this tonight?

"But why, O preacher, do this tonight?" I hear your heart ask such question. I answer, for every good reason do this tonight, and for no reason thinkable should you delay it till tomorrow. Tomorrow is not yours. Tomorrow may not be yours at all. It is forbidden you to put this matter off till tomorrow. "Boast not thyself of tomorrow, for thou knowest not what a day may bring forth." Today, if you hear His voice, harden not your heart. You are not even to think of tomorrow. Christ's time is today. Christ's call is today. Your need is today. Your duty is today. Your danger is today. Christ says: "Close in with Me today." Do you say, "Yes, I will; I do tonight." You will, then, tonight be saved. O God, bring the lost ones to Thyself just now!

There is yet another manifestation of faith in this nobleman's case. When he went on down the way that led him home, the servants met him before he reached home, and they began their glad story: "Master, the boy is well." He said, "When did the change come?" And they said, "Yesterday, at the seventh hour, the fever left him." "So the father knew that it was at the same hour in the which Jesus said unto him, 'Thy son liveth'; and himself believed, and his whole house." That is the last stage of faith. That is assurance. He came and he saw. There was the lad back from the gates of death, sound and well. That was a happy home, you may be sure. You may be sure that father told them over and over again what Jesus said, and how He looked, and everything that pertained to the vast matter. What joy they must have had as they talked about Him! And they all believed, and doubtless said, "He shall have our trust, our service, and our love, all the days of our life. We know that He is God, even our God forever." That is the last stage of faith.

The trouble with sinners is that they wish this last part first. They wish assurance first. They feel and in their hearts say that if Christ would give them to feel this or that, if He would fill their hearts with peace and joy, they would then trust Him. Trust Him without any such dictation. You must put your case into Christ's hands and leave it there. Yours it is to give up to Jesus. Yours it is to decide for Jesus. Yours it is to choose Jesus. Yours it is to say: "Lord Jesus, I don't ask Thee to wait on me another hour; sometime and somewhere I have meant to settle this question; I won't ask for more time; I will settle it tonight; I will take Thee at Thy Word; I surrender now, and forever, to Thee." If you will do that tonight, you shall be saved tonight.

O soul, wrong with God, take this great step tonight. Take it before we go from this service. What is the essence of faith? The very essence of faith is that the soul will willingly give up to the will of Christ. You are already in Christ's hands, O sinner. You are as much in His hands as is the Christian. What is the difference, then? The Christian is in His hands willingly. "Have Thy way with me, take the reins of my life and govern me ever as Thou wishest." That is the spirit of a Christian. Say tonight, O lost one, "Lord, Thy way shall be mine, Thy will shall be mine; I give up to Thee tonight, a poor, needy sinner; I wish to be a Christian; Thou must make me one, and Thou hast said if I would come to Thee that Thou wouldst not cast me out; I come now." Won't you do this now? In this last moment, for in a moment we must go; won't you close in with Jesus now? Think about going out tonight with your heart against Him! Oh, the wrong and the peril of it all, waiting until some other time! Won't you tonight close in with Jesus, and tonight say "Yes" to Him, and tonight give up to Him forever? You remember the story of the magistrate, Archias, of the city of Thebes. He was going out one night to a place of feasting and revelry, and one of his faithful servants intercepted him on his way, and slipped into his hand a note. Archias said, "What is it about?" And the servant said, "About a very serious matter, O prince; be sure to read it before you go to that place." And the prince thrust it down into his pocket, unread, muttering: "Serious matters later, but none tonight for me!" And he went, unheeding, on, and serious matters did come later. The letter was a disclosure of a plot that the servant had discovered that enemies had laid to take that prince's life that night, and the faithful servant had thus warned him to stay away from that place of conspiracy and probable death. But the prince did not heed the message: did not even read it, and came to most serious issues, even to death, that night, from that delay.

O soul, do you wish to be a Christian? Do you, my boy over there, and you, my young man over there, whose heart has been touched again and again with the call of the gospel? Do you wish to be a Christian? Do you wish to be tonight? Listen once more: "Him that cometh to Me, I will in no wise cast out." Come now to Him, yield yourself to Him, receive Him to be your personal Savior, and you shall go out of this house saved. We are going to pray that you may settle it right now. Let every head be bowed, and for a few moments let us pray in silence. Lord, teach us how to pray!

9
Christ's Message to the Weak

A bruised reed shall He not break, and smoking flax
shall He not quench, till He send forth judgment unto victory
(Matt. 12:20).

The context was read a few moments ago that you might see how this strange language came to be used. Jesus went on the Sabbath day, with His disciples, through the cornfield, and, being hungry, they began to pluck the ears of corn and to eat. This called forth the very censorious criticism of the Pharisees, who all through the Savior's public ministry sought to find fault with what He said and did. He called to their remembrance that incident of the olden times when David went into the house of God and did eat the shewbread, which was not lawful for him to eat, nor for them who were with him, but lawful only for the priests to eat, and David was justified in doing it. And then Jesus announced that the Son of Man was Lord even of the Sabbath day. And next, Jesus went into their temple, where there was a man with a withered hand, and these same carping Pharisees asked Him if it was right to heal on the Sabbath day, that they might accuse Him. He answered them by asking this question:"If one of you shall have a sheep, and if it shall fall into a pit on the Sabbath day, will you wait until the next day to get it out? How much then is a man better than a sheep? Wherefore, I say unto you, it is lawful to do well on the Sabbath day." Then He said to the man, "Stretch forth thine hand." And he stretched it forth and it was made whole, like as the other.

The indignation of the Pharisees had passed beyond all limits now, and they went out and held a council against Him, how they might destroy Him. And as He withdrew from that place, the multitudes followed Him, and especially those that were favorable to Him, bringing to Him their troubled and their diseased and their sick, and He healed them all. He quoted to them the prophecy of Isaiah, made long before, descriptive of the character of the Messiah when He should appear among men. The concluding part of that description is the strange language we have this morning for a text:"A bruised reed shall He not break, and smoking flax shall He not quench, till He send forth judgment unto victory."

Criticism is, I fear, a very common and dangerous sin. I speak, of course, of uncharitable criticism, of censorious criticism, of carping and fault-finding and misjudging. That is a very common sin, I fear, and surely it is a very dangerous sin. Many a wound is received into many a life because some word was spoken that was uncharitable, unjust, unkind, un-Christian, which wound is carried to the grave. Jesus put His mighty protest against that kind of thing. Do you not recall that when He came down to the closing part of His marvelous sermon on the mount He talked like this:"Judge not, that ye be not judged. For with what judgment ye judge, ye shall be judged; and with what measure ye mete, it shall be measured to you again." And then He asks:"Why beholdest thou the mote"— a mote is a little splinter, a tiny splinter—"Why beholdest thou the tiny splinter that is in thy brother's eye, and considerest not the beam"—a beam is a great log—"considerest not the great log that is in thine own eye?" And then He uses terrific words:"Thou hypocrite! First cast out the beam"—the great log—"out of thine own eye; and then shalt thou see clearly to cast out the mote"—the little splinter—"out of thy brother's eye." What a mighty protest the Savior here brings against all uncharitable criticism! Now that strange setting was given this text. Criticism harsh and reviling, and censorious, and untrue, gathered around the life and works of Jesus, and He made response to it one day on the occasion of the text, quoting in His response the description given of Him by Isaiah long before, as the prophet foretold the character of the coming One who should be the world's Savior and King.

What then is the meaning of the text? In its deep meaning, its teaching plainly seems to be that the reign of Jesus Christ in this world is a reign of gentleness and compassion and forbearance and patience and tenderness and love. Its teaching is that while Jesus Christ is a lion to devour His adversaries, He is at the same time a lamb, even the Lamb of God, who will take away the sin of every soul that will only venture to surrender utterly to Him. The teaching of the text is that while Jesus Christ came into this world to destroy the works of the devil, which destruction, thank God, shall be ultimately and effectually accomplished, yet He came at the same time to save poor devil-deceived and devil-driven souls, if only out of the depths of repentant hearts they will look unto Him.

Those two little metaphors that He employs are very suggestive. He talks about the bruised reed and about the smoking flax. Oh, what a glorious teacher was Jesus! Every teacher ought daily to study His method. He took up the simple things of life, the things about which the people knew, and from these He drew lessons which He proclaimed to the people, so that their deep meaning would more and more and more appear out of these simple matters to the understanding of listening minds and hearts. So here in the text the illustrations are exceedingly simple. He talks about the bruised reed and about the smoking flax. These are indeed very little and insignificant things. The reed was the little musical instrument employed by the shepherd as he led his flocks over hill and vale. As he blew upon that little reed, with its simple indentures, the reed which corresponds to the cane that grows on our river banks, the shepherd's simple music was thus discoursed. That reed after a while became bruised, and then the shepherd threw it down to be trodden under foot of men and beasts. And Jesus' word was this: "I will not break the bruised reed." And He talked about the smoking flax. The writers on Oriental customs tell us that the smoking flax was something that corresponds to the little wick that you have seen put down into a vessel of oil or grease, one end of which is ignited and gives out light. That light may be blown out, and yet the flax continues to smoke. Jesus took that simple illustration and said, "I will not quench the smoking flax."

Let us see if we may not learn today something of the wondrous tenderness and good cheer in these simple illustrations employed by the Savior.

First of all, they suggest weakness. Jesus does not cast us off and destroy us because of our weakness. Oh, how weak we are! What is weaker than a little bruised reed? What is weaker than that little smoking flax? Now out of those little ordinary illustrations the Master would teach us a wonderful lesson for the cheer of our oft dispirited hearts and for the strengthening of our wearied, driven lives. Look at ourselves in any way that we may, and our painful weakness will be discovered to us.

Oh, how weak we are in knowledge! How little we know! How little we know about anything! How little we know about ourselves, about God, about God's word! How little we know about His providence! How little we know about the great, deep, blessed mysteries of grace! Oh, wondrous truth, He does not cast us off, even though we are so weak in knowledge!

And how weak we are in faith! You and I, assembled for the simple service of this Lord's Day morning, ought to believe more profoundly in Jesus Christ than did the men who saw Him after He had risen from the dead. We ought today to believe more in Jesus than did Thomas, who, when he looked upon Jesus, cried out: "My Lord, and my God." Nineteen hundred years of Christian history are behind us. Thomas and his fellow disciples were in the beginning of the Christian era. We have seen our Lord's Word put to every possible test. We have seen every doctrine of that Book pounded upon with all the forces of evil known to men and demons, and yet the Book stands, more immovable and impregnable than Gibraltar. We have more right to believe on Jesus Christ today than the men who saw Him after He had come from the dead, and who journeyed those forty days with Him, as He yet further revealed the mysteries of His kingdom. And yet how painfully weak we are in faith! Take such a promise as this: "If two of you shall agree on earth as touching anything that they shall ask, it shall be done for them of My Father which is in heaven." And still we cower, and falter, and are impotent, are unbelieving before a promise like that. And yet, thank God, He does not cast us off.

How weak we are, too, in resisting temptation! Wasn't it Mr. Spurgeon, who said that there is a back door to every heart, and if Satan fails to get in at the front door, then he enters in at the back door? When we see him coming to the front door, we sometimes arm ourselves and resist him, because we are steadfast in the faith. This is the victory that overcometh the world, and Satan too, even our faith. We sometimes see Satan coming, and we resist him earnestly, looking unto God for wisdom and help, and thus is Satan beaten back, even as Goliath was vanquished by David of old. Then we felicitate ourselves upon our splendid achievement, and ere we are aware, Satan has gone around and come in at the back door, and stormed the very citadel of our being; and we have been caught in his snare and have gone down into temptation and sin. Thank God, He does not cast us off utterly, leaving us without hope, even though we do that!

And then, how weak we are when we are called upon to endure afflictions. Oh, how we chafe and fume and fret and worry under life's afflictions, not laying to heart the gracious promises of God concerning them! Take such a promise as this: "For our light affliction, which is but for a moment, worketh for us a far more exceeding and eternal weight of glory." Or take this: "And we know that all things work together for good to them that love God, to them who are the called according to His purpose." And yet we chafe and fume and worry over the afflictions of life, which afflictions are often God's disciplinary chastisements to humble us, and to conquer our selfishness, and to win us away from the things that harm us, and to bring us closer to heaven and to Christ.

And then how weak we are in zeal. One of the most heart-breaking things on this earth is the weakness of God's people in their zeal for Him. Why will any of God's children ever walk in a course of life that could at all suggest the compromise of their Lord? Why will they do it? How can they do it? Yet they do those very things. O brethren, blessed be the mercy of God, that though we are weak in faith, though we are weak in knowledge, though we are weak in the resistance of temptation, though we are weak in standing up for Jesus, the very thing we are left in the world to do, yet He does not cast us off!

Nor is that all. These two little illustrations suggest a still deeper truth. Jesus does not cast His people off, even though seemingly their lives may be worthless. That bruised reed seems to be a worthless thing. The shepherd has got it bruised, and no longer does it discourse music for him, and he throws it down to be trampled under foot of man and beast. Jesus takes it up, turns it into an illustration, and points a profoundly cheering lesson for the tempted and weak. Christ does not throw His blood-bought child away, even though he may be weak, and even though, to human appearances, he may sometimes be worthless. Frequently, we raise the question: "Now, what good am I, anyway, in the kingdom of God? I can see how that preacher is accomplishing something; I can see how that Sunday school worker is bringing something graciously to pass. But, oh, what good am I?" O sir, if you are a regenerated child of God, He will not cast you off; He will not cast you off. "I will not break the bruised reed."

Nor is that all. These illustrations would suggest that sometimes we reach the place, not only of weakness in the kingdom of God, and not only of seeming worthlessness in the kingdom of God, but where our lives seem positively offensive in the kingdom of God, and yet He does not utterly cast off such worthless ones.

I doubt if I am speaking to a single Christian parent here today whose Christian course, at some time or another, has not been grievously offensive in the kingdom of God. Why were you not cast off? Because of the infinite mercy of God. That is the reason why the backslider, the really saved soul that was tempted and seduced away from holiness and righteousness, is not finally lost. Jesus Christ will not quench the smoking flax. The greatest comfort in the world for the backslider is wrapped up in this scriptural truth. Jesus will not quench the smoking flax. Why? Down underneath that little smoking flax there is some fire. There would not be smoke unless there was some fire. It may be just a little fire, but there is some, and Jesus will not quench that little, tiny, smoking spark. Sometimes, oft-times, our lives seem only to be smoking things for God. Yet He will kindle that little spark of fire underneath the smoke, and will cause the wick to be lighted again; and this lighted wick may yet kindle a great conflagration. Oh, there are worlds of comfort here for the return of the backslidden Christian!

Now what is the gracious encouragement of this text for Christ's people? Here it is, as I see it. The encouragement of this text for Christ's people is that the least little Christian in the world is as really saved as is the greatest, so far as his salvation is concerned, so far as his regeneration is concerned, so far as his justification is concerned. But, so far as his happiness is concerned, so far as his usefulness is concerned, so far as his joy is concerned, so far as his peace is concerned, that is another question. There are degrees of peace and joy and happiness in the Christian life. But the teaching of this text, borne out by God's Word, is that the salvation of the least little Christian in the world is as certain a fact as is the salvation of Paul, or of Abraham, or of any other who has mightily influenced the world for the divine glory and for human good. Now, do you know a sublimer truth than that? Do you, O Christian, know any sweeter truth than that the least little Christian cleansed by the blood of Christ is as thoroughly saved and will as certainly get to heaven as the greatest Christian on the face of the earth? In the true believer there is planted an incorruptible seed which liveth and abideth forever. Oh, isn't that glorious?

Now, why is that so? That is so because this little Christian, first of all, cost the Lord Jesus Christ just as much as the big one cost Him. This little Christian had the same price paid for his redemption as had the mightiest Christian who ever testified for Jesus. This little Christian, I say, cost our Lord just as much as did the biggest. Sometimes we have heard a song that went something like this:

> One drop of the blood, one drop of the blood,
>   He shed upon Calvary's brow,
> Will cleanse me from sin and free me within
>   And make me e'en whiter than snow.

The song is not a good one. It does not convey the truth, just as some other sweet sounding songs do not convey the truth. Every drop of the blood poured out from all those gaping wounds in His dear body was for me. That agony of the cross, all that desolation, that loneliness, those quivering limbs, that falling blood, all of it, all of it, was for me. Jesus Christ did not die for men in the bulk, but He died for the individual. "The Son of God who loved me, and gave Himself for me." I cost my Lord all of Gethsemane and all of Calvary. I cost Him as much as did Paul. He paid the same price for the least one in His kingdom as for the greatest.

Nor is that all. Jesus Christ will see to the certain salvation of the least little Christian as well as the greatest, because He does the saving. Oh, precious truth, most glorious doctrine—salvation is by grace. The least saint in His kingdom will be as certainly saved as the greatest, because the salvation of both is by grace. "By grace are ye saved, through faith, and that not of yourselves; it is the gift of God, not of works, lest any man should boast." And so that little, timid, shrinking Christian, daring hardly to venture the public confession that he believes on Christ, yet if he does really believe on Him, he is as thoroughly saved as the mighty Christian who shouts, "I know that my Redeemer liveth," because Jesus does the saving of them both. Marvelous comfort is this for the timid children of God! It is the testimony of God's word. "My sheep hear My voice, and I know them, and they follow Me. And I give unto them eternal life; and they shall never perish, neither shall any man pluck them out of My hand. My Father, which gave them Me, is greater than all; and no man is able to pluck them out of My Father's hand. I and My Father are one." Oh, there is a cable that Satan will never break, never! Never in perdition will Satan shout:

"Here is one who once was saved through Jesus' blood." Never! Satan may harm our influence. He may do terrible hurt to our happiness. He may afflict us with many sorrows here. But never will he hold a banquet in hell over the blood-washed child of God! Tell it everywhere; the least little Christian is as really saved as is the greatest and the happiest and the most useful. "Blessed be the God and Father of our Lord Jesus Christ, who hath begotten us again into a lively hope, to an inheritance incorruptible, and undefiled, and that fadeth not away, reserved in heaven for you who are kept by the power of God through faith unto salvation, ready to be revealed in the last time." Isn't it glorious? Salvation, not of human works, salvation by the infinite grace of Almighty God! O brethren, it is the sweetest thing I ever heard in this world, salvation through the grace of God. Christ's work of salvation is sure. Yonder, in my native state of North Carolina, when the railroad came through those towering mountains, the Appalachian range, some years ago, it wound around mountainsides and went over yawning chasms, and through tunnels, and by the edges of awful precipices. If the train had turned just an inch or two, it would have gone over with all the passengers, hundreds of feet below, and dashed them to instant death. One day the engineer took his wife and little son into the engine with him, as they made that run from Asheville to Murphy. And the little son, five years old, laughed with delight as he looked out of that window at the yawning chasms and fearful precipices. The mother after a while said, "Son, aren't you afraid? If this train were to jump off this track we would be dashed to death, all of us, in one minute. Aren't you afraid?" And with perfect assurance the little man answered, "No, Mama, I am not afraid because my papa is running this engine." Glory be to God, Jesus Christ guides the engine of the car of salvation! There will be no collisions and there will be no wrecks. There will be no dashing over the precipices to the rocks of eternal death for anyone who has surely rested his case for salvation upon the Son of God. Do you see that ship yonder on the sea? See how it tosses. A great storm is sweeping the sea. Do you see the ship far out there, many hundreds of miles in mid-ocean? Do you not also see the angry clouds, and do you not hear the awful roar of thunder? On that ship is an old captain, quietly sitting at the helm, smoking with perfect compla- cency. He is not afraid. On that same ship is a little girl, an orphan child, of a dozen years, crossing the ocean to loved ones yonder where she can have a home, because her own parents are dead. The timid girl of a dozen years is on the sea for the first time. The child trembles and sobs and wrings her hands, she is so distressed. But is not the child's life as safe as that of the quiet captain? She is on the same ship. O brothers, we live because we are in Christ. If you are just in Christ, your salvation is an absolute certainty. Some time ago a pastor found himself on the outskirts of the city, making pastoral calls, as night came on. As he turned homeward, he was attracted by what seemed to be the sobs of a child. It was even so. A little lad had lost his way. The older boys had taken him there, had purposely left the little fellow, and he did not know how to get home and night was coming on. The pastor, as he drove along, heard the sobs, found the little fellow, and listened to his story. The boys had taken him out there and had left him. The pastor said, after he heard it all, "Will you trust me to take you home?" The little fellow came out from under the electric light and searchingly looked up into the preacher's face. What should he do? He had been deceived once. But after searching the preacher's face with his little earnest eyes for a moment, he said, "Yes, sir, you may take me home." The little fellow knew the street and number. The preacher took him home. The mother was already distraught with unspeakable anx- iety for the little thing that was missing. And when the preacher took the little thing to the door, the mother was overwhelmed with joy as she clasped the child to her heart and thanked the preacher. What if that preacher had stopped when he got the little one half- way home, and had left the little fellow to whatever fate might hap- pen to him? O sirs, will Jesus Christ begin the work of salvation in a human soul and abandon that soul? Never, forever! "He which hath begun a good work in you will perform it until the day of Jesus Christ."

How long is this blessed preservation to continue? "A bruised reed shall He not break, and smoking flax shall He not quench, till

He send forth judgment unto victory." There is to be "victory." That is a noble word, and nobler still when applied to the triumph of God's grace in a believer's heart. Yonder lay General Wolfe dying on the Heights of Abraham, wounded to death in the fearful battle. They laid his mortally wounded body under a tree, and while his life-blood ebbed away, as he lay there attended by two of his men, they heard shouts on the field, and the shout was: "They fly, they fly." And the dying Wolfe, arousing himself from his death struggle, said, "Who is it that flies?" And they said, "General, the enemy flies." Then clasping his hands, he said, barely able to be heard, "Victory! I die happy." O my brothers, it is victory for the soul that surely relies upon Jesus Christ. It is victory here, and hereafter. The white hairs of these men and women tell us that soon, ah, too soon, we must follow them yonder to the grave, and they shall sleep with their fathers. But it is victory for them. Is there anything more beautifully glorious than a ripe old Christian waiting for the summons to go home? It is victory for these middle-aged men and women, out in the thick of the battle, driven and beaten and tossed. Oh, it is victory, so far as your salvation is concerned, if you are hidden with Christ. It is victory for these young Christians. Oh, how Satan does his utmost to delude the human soul on this vital point. A thousand times, I dare say, men have said to me, "I would like to be a Christian, but I am afraid that I could not hold out long." I answer, "You cannot hold out until sundown, you cannot hold out five minutes, you cannot hold out sixty seconds." Christ holds the soul that surrenders to Him. Christ comes in and reinforces it. Christ has been formed within such soul the hope of glory, and greater is He that is in you than he that is in the world. Oh, that we may be clear on this vital point as we deal with lost men. They cannot live the Christian life, if left to themselves, for one hour. See how Paul put it: "I know whom I have believed, and am persuaded that He is able to keep that which I have committed unto Him against that day."

My message is done and my hour is gone. What about it all? My closing word to these Christians, first of all, is that they be happy today in the precious thought that they are saved. Have you really surrendered to Christ? If yes, then we will walk the heavenly street together. Have you received Jesus Christ to be your Savior? "I am persuaded that neither death, nor life, nor angels, nor principalities, nor powers, nor things present, nor things to come, nor height, nor depth, nor any other creature shall be able to separate us from the love of God which is in Christ Jesus our Lord." Oh, just sit down, this blessed Lord's Day, and ponder this precious truth: "I am saved, I am saved, thank God, I am saved!" Do I speak to some who are unhappy, some backslidden souls, some lukewarm, indifferent Christians, some who are among the fleshpots of Egypt, some who are not living up to their privileges? Then I would bring you back to consider afresh the vital question whether you have really taken Jesus to be your Savior. Oh, let us be clear on this point. O backslider, who in the other days had joy and peace in your Christian living, and now the heavens seem like brass, come back today, confessing your sins and yielding yourself afresh to this all-merciful Savior. O soul, neglecting your duty to Christ, come back today! O church member, not in conscious fellowship with Jesus, come back today. Come and confess your backslidings and sins, and He will surely heal you. Come back. You ought to do it today. Act this morning upon His blessed promise: "If we confess our sins, He is faithful and just to forgive us our sins, and to cleanse us from all unrighteousness."

10

The Conquering
Hosts of God

*And when the servant of the man of God was risen early, and
gone forth, behold, a host compassed the city both with horses and
chariots. And his servant said unto him, Alas, my master! how
shall we do? And he answered, Fear not: for they that be with us
are more than they that be with them. And Elisha prayed, and
said, Lord, I pray Thee, open his eyes that he may see. And the
Lord opened the eyes of the young man and he saw; and, behold,
the mountain was full of horses and chariots of fire round about
Elisha (2 Kgs. 6:15, 16, 17).*

The text calls our attention to one of the most interesting events in all the Old Testament Scriptures. There are several remarkably interesting events
connected with the life of this man Elisha. This one we are now to
consider is one of the most beautiful, one of the most instructive,
and one of the most comforting for the people of God. Here in the
text are two men, poles apart in their feeling and in their spirit. One
is swept with consternation and fear, and the other is perfectly calm
and tranquil. The one is dismayed by the prospects of harm from

the enemies about them. The other calmly looks above all the dust and tumult of earth and sees and trusts One able and ready, and certain to take care of His people. The latter man is steadfast in faith, which faith God's children ought ever to bear towards Him. The former is held terribly in the grip of material things and earthly surroundings and thus comes short of the privileges of the lofty and conquering faith the child of God ought to have.

The text strikingly suggests a lesson that needs always to be laid to heart, and that lesson is that God's presence with His people is not a mere theory, but a most glorious fact. Our theory, to be sure, is that God is with His people. We delight to say that He does not leave them in the sixth trouble, nor forsake them in the seventh; that He never fails nor forsakes. That is our theory. The truth of this Scripture mightily brings out the lesson that the theory is a fact; a fact that can be relied upon; the most certain fact in the life of God's child; the fact that never fails. Yes, God is with His people. They may rely upon it. He never fails nor forsakes them. He does keep His word to His people.

Many striking lessons are suggested by this old-time incident. Some of these lessons I desire to consider with you today. The first is, God's presence with His people is not realized by the enemies of God and His people. This truth is forcefully brought out in the context. The king of Syria, Ben-hadad, utterly forgot to reckon upon God when he was making war against Israel's king and prophet and people. Men always miss it to the last degree who do not reckon upon God. God's enemies, who are likewise the enemies of His people, fail at this point, which is a vital point. They do not reckon upon God's presence with His people. That illustration finds the most striking expression in this old-time story. The king of Syria was bent on doing destruction to the king and country of Israel. So he laid the finest plans and gave himself to the most splendid military tactics to destroy the king of Israel and the people of Israel, and yet he found himself every time foiled. His best-laid plans came to naught. He went down every time in defeat. His shrewdly laid plans, when he came to the execution of them, were all utterly futile. His projects to surround the king and his army were somehow always baffled. When, again and again, he pursued his well-laid plan, supposing that this time he had the king in a net, the king was not there, neither were his men. So, by and by, the king of Syria, in great disappointment, and with heart much piqued, called his men together and said, "What man do I have who is for the king of Israel? There must be some traitor in my camp. Now, who is it?" And one of them answered back, "Not at all, O king. Your diagnosis is incorrect. It is not some man in your army that is making the trouble for you. God has a man on the other side, one man, and all your secrets, whispered in your bedchamber, God communicates to that prophet, Elisha, and the prophet communicates them to the king, and when you are just ready to take them in your net, they are not there to be taken. That is the explanation." And then the king said, "Where is he? I will make short work of him. If he be the hindrance, then the hindrance shall be removed. Let that man be found." And so the king gathers about him a great army, and he sends them forth by night to surround this prophet, this one lone prophet, as he was in Dothan. The whole army is to surround him, and then with the coming of the morning to capture him.

What a tribute the bad man unconsciously pays to the good man! Think of sending a great army after one man! Think of sending horses and chariots and a great host, with all the accouterments of war, after one lone man! Yet that is the tribute that the bad man pays to the good man. All along the bad man feels the emanations from the good man of an influence, invisible and subtle, yet strangely mighty, and this, time and again, strikes terror to the bad man's heart, as well it may. It was that same feeling that provoked bloody Queen Mary to say on one occasion: "I fear the prayers of John Knox more than I fear an army of ten thousand men." There was something in John Knox, the outflowing of which smote terror to the heart of the cruel queen. So, also, this wicked king unconsciously pays a marvelous tribute to this man of God. He sends a great army, equipped with all the equipments of war, to startle and terrify and to capture the plain, simple prophet of God.

Now, the folly of this man is the folly of every other bad man. The extreme folly of this Syrian king was that he did not reckon upon God. This the enemies of God fail to do all along. This was the mistake made by Edward, the king of England. When Edward, king of England, rode out before the Scottish troops before the battle of Bannockburn, he said to the great general who rode along by his side: "Why, there is just a handful of those fellows, and we have an army that are as the sands of the sea for multitude. There is just a handful of those men. Do they mean to fight us?" Then in a moment more all those Scottish troops kneeled down in plain sight of the army of Edward, and the general who rode alongside Edward said, "See, king. Yon men who pray will win the day or they will die." They reckoned on God, while King Edward and his hosts left Him out. Bad men, all along, are failing to reckon upon God, and are thus making their everlasting mistake. That has been the ruinous mistake of the persecutor through the generations. The man who thinks to undo God's work by swords, by implements of war, by carnal weapons, the man who thinks to do that, fails sooner or later, and fails utterly. He always fails, as surely he ought to fail. With pardonable pride my Baptist people may point to one record, and that is that never in all the stretch of centuries did Baptists persecute for religion's sake. Here is one chaplet of glory men will never take from the brow of my beloved people. We have always contended that every man must be allowed to worship God without restraint or proscription. We have contended that the thumbscrew and the rack and the tortures of the Inquisition and every conceivable expression of persecution are all utterly inimical to God's spirit and to God's plan. But the bad man forgets that God will not have His people to trust in carnal weapons. That would be for them to compromise His spirit and His purpose and His revelation to man.

Here, then, is the mistake of the persecutor always. It was the mistake of Pharaoh when he oppressed Israel in Egypt. Pharaoh did not reckon upon God. Moses said, "You had better take God into your plans." Moses said, "You must sooner or later consciously come into direct dealing with Him." Moses said, "You may not always trifle with Him with impunity." Moses said, "There is a pay-day coming." Moses said, "O king, you had better consider Him who sits in the heavens, unto whom all men must answer. You had better reckon upon Him." But Pharaoh scouted it all and scorned it all and laughed at it all. But one dark night the death-dealing messenger, God's angel, marched up and down the borders of Egypt, and when the morning came, the wailing land of Egypt, from border to border, sounded out the desolate cry of uncounted hosts, because the first-born in every house lay dead. Then the king's heart relented and he said, "There is a God, and I cannot trifle with Him." That was the trouble with Herod, who had the Innocents put to death—thinking thus to foil the purpose of God. Herod thought that by sword, by fasces, by carnal weapons, he could obliterate the kingdom of God. That way has always failed. When they have applied the torch to one child of God, persecuting him to death, burning him at the stake for religion's sake, out of the ashes have come troops of Christians who said, "We believe what that man believes whom you have just burned to death. We are ready to be burned for the same thing." And when they have drowned some man in the same spirit, out of the gurgling waters have come ten thousand men, and they have said, "Drown us. We believe the same thing."

The bad man fails to reckon upon God and is doomed. The king of the olden days left God out of his plans and was doomed. Every such man is doomed. Poor Voltaire left God out of his plans, utterly scouted the doctrines of God, scouted them so completely as to say, "In a little while there will not be a Bible left, nor a Christian." He printed that direful prophecy on his printing-press. See what has come to pass. God's people have captured that printing-press that today prints this blessed Word of God, and the house in which poor Voltaire lived is now, they tell us, a great Bible store from which are scattered everywhere the leaves from the Book of Life. Poor Tom Paine, whose writings have harmed so many young men—poor Paine said in 1809: "In one hundred years there will not be a Bible left." The one hundred years are barely gone, but more than twenty times the number of Bibles that the people ever heard of before have been printed and scattered over the world since that direful prophecy. He did not reckon upon God. Poor Ingersoll, who went up and down this great country, lecturing to large audiences with his striking wit and sarcasm, building

up men of straw to knock them down—on the very spot where he
wrote his lecture which he was pleased to style: "The Mistakes of
Moses," on that very spot they have built a noble house of worship,
open every day in the week and every week in the year, in which
building scores and hundreds and thousands every year hear of God
and many believe and live.

Every man who leaves God out of his reckoning comes to desolation. The businessman who leaves Him out will come to defeat.
That was the significance of that parable which Jesus spoke to us
about the rich man. He wished to build great barns because the old
barns were inadequate. He would fill them with his harvests, and
then be ready for every exigency. But in the unexpected hour, in
the very heyday of his glory, when he was on the pinnacle of his
splendid worldly achievement, God suddenly took him in hand,
with the awful statement: "This night thy life shall be required of
thee, thou fool." Men who do not reckon upon God come to just
such destruction. So it was with the king of Syria. So it always is.
So it ever shall be.

Let us study a second lesson suggested by the text. It is that
God's presence is often not realized by His servant. It is altogether
probable that this nameless servant of Elisha was a Christian. He was
daily with the prophet of God. He ministered to him. They were
close companions. It is probable, therefore, that this servant of Elisha was a Christian. But note the contrast between the two men.
The servant was swept with fear. Apprehension seized him. Awful
dismay possessed him as he looked around one morning and saw
the city surrounded with horses and chariots and a great host of soldiers, with all the implements of war. He came back to the prophet
with the cry: "Alas, my master, how shall we do?" Now see how the
prophet spoke: "Fear not, for they that be with us are more than
they that be with them." "Why, there are just two of us, Master,"
cries the servant; "there are just two of us, and there are thousands
of them; what can we do?" And the prophet makes some such reply
as this: "There is One, an invisible One, and that One counteth
more in the carrying forward of the cause of right than all the ar-
mored battalions of men that can ever make their tramp felt in all

the world." Then the prophet prays, "O God, open his eyes that he may see; just let the young man see." And the Lord opened his eyes and behold, the mountains were filled with horses and chariots of fire round about the two men.

Oh, that is a faithful picture of the situation today! How like Elisha's servant are we all at times! We look and we see the horses and the chariots and the marvelous display of carnal weapons, and we feel, "Alas, who are we, and what can we do in the presence of such foes and forces?" And the more that we cherish such a spirit, the more easily may the enemies of God triumph over us. The awful problem, the awful sin with the people of God, is their behavior like unto the behavior of Elisha's servant. Take our many fears. How fearful we can be! How easily dismayed we can become! What terrific apprehensions do we allow, at times, to possess us! What darts of trouble we see flying around us! Oh, what moaning winds come to us! And we say, "Things are just awful, just simply awful!" Things are not awful at all while God is with us.

Someone put it right when he said that even God's people insist on having a trouble factory in their houses, and if trouble does not come along naturally, they put the factory to work and make it come. We somehow imagine that this is a part of the Christian program, that we should be cast down with trouble. I think I have told some of you at the prayer-meeting of an experience elsewhere, where time and again I called to see an old woman, who was very well-to-do, who had a magnificent bank account, large plantations, splendid material possessions; and every time I visited her she dealt out to me the sad story of her apprehensions and fears. She was afraid somebody would get that bank stock. She was afraid somebody would manipulate her out of those great plantations, and out of that splendid home left her by her husband. She was afraid that at last the outcome would be for her that she would have to die in a poorhouse. I heard that as long as I could, and at last I ventured to say, "Well, my good woman, what if you do have to die in the poorhouse? What does that signify? If you are God's child, as you say, His convoy of angels would as surely meet you there, to carry you up to the heavenly heights, as they would call for you were you in the splendid palace." How she did dishonor God by all such talk.

I knew another Christian who, every time the spring came, could see hobgoblins and specters and ghosts. It was the year when there was not going to be any rain; certain not to be any rain that year. It was the year when the farmers would not make any corn. It was the year when the wheat was all going to rust. It was the year—you could see the signs now—when the boll-weevil was going to get all the cotton. I have heard him talk like that for years and years. And every such word was to the dishonor of God. There is your man playing the act of Elisha's nameless servant, and saying, "Master, we are done for. We have at last come to the bottom of the ditch." He is leaving God out. The man who applies that principle in Christian life and work is Elisha's servant over again.

Whenever a man knows his duty he is to do that duty. He is unhesitatingly to do that duty, and God will take care of the results. I saw a man join the church once in another city. He was converted graciously, and he was a magnificent man, but he said, "I cannot join the church here. If I join a church, I must move somewhere else. I cannot join here." And why such a conclusion, he was asked. And then he narrated the story of a difficulty between him and a man in the church. Their difficulty was supposed to be serious, very serious. Who was to blame, I do not know, nor care—perhaps both were to blame. He said, "The years—many of them—have gone since the difficulty, and we have never looked into each other's faces, and we have never presumed to speak to each other. I wish I could be in the church, but it is unthinkable that I should, under the circumstances, offer to join this church and expect to be received." I could easily meet that argument, and did so with the doctrine of individual responsibility to God. He said, "Well, what might happen if I offered to join the church?" I said, "That is not your lookout. That is God's lookout. Your business is to do your duty, to walk down the aisle like a man for God, with the inflexible purpose to obey God and leave all the results with Him." At the very next service he stood up and said, "I have made my surrender to God. Men and brethren, I wish to be with you in the church; if you feel willing, I would be glad to have a place with you." The first man to get his hand was the man who had not spoken to him in a dozen years, and in one minute the family feud was at an end. We see specters and hobgoblins and all sorts of difficulties when we do not see God; but, my brethren, when we just admit God upon the premises, then our difficulties vanish like the clouds before the all-glorious sun. God forgive our unbelief! How it hinders His work, and how we let our fears, like those ten spies in Joshua's time, paralyze our faith and our powers.

There is another lesson in the text I would briefly mention. There was one man here who was true and who saw God. The true servant of God always sees Him. Elisha was the true servant of God, and he saw God. Oh! Isn't it sublime how Elisha behaved himself when the servant said, "This city is surrounded by armed men. We are at our wit's end!" "What do I care for the armed men?" replies the prophet. "God is my refuge and strength, an ever present help in time of trouble." There was God's man. He was like his predecessor, Elijah, on Carmel's height, when he and the hosts of Baal met in the one great decisive test as to who was the true God. I need not here recite the familiar and wonderful story.

Elisha is walking worthily in the footsteps of his predecessor. So he says in effect to the young man, "Why, young man, how much do you count God for—God's interest in His children, and in His cause, and in His chosen people over whom He watches more tenderly than a mother watches over her children? Young man, how much do you count Him for?" Isn't it a thrilling spectacle—the spectacle of a man who believes God and ever strives just to do His will? See Abraham. God said: "Go, Abraham." "Where?" "Never mind; go." And Abraham went out, not knowing whither he went, perfectly peaceful, perfectly satisfied. "I have the mandate of heaven's King behind me and it is all right. I am going through an untrodden wilderness, but it is all right. I know not where I shall land, I know not the outcome, but it is all right." When God said, "Offer Isaac on the altar," it was all right. It was all right because the chief factor in his life was God.

See Nehemiah. He was a serious patriot, a true reformer, a genuine man. He is to rebuild the walls of Jerusalem, but he is an exile. With no resources but his faith in God, he goes to his great task. Though laughed at, sneered at, joked about, on and on he goes. He tells us why: "The God of heaven, He shall prosper this work that I am trying to do." So it always goes with the man who just believes and obeys God. O brethren, if only our eyes were opened what might we not see!

That remarkable Sunday school worker, who passed to heaven a little while ago, Dr. H. Clay Trumbull, tells in one of his books of this scene that occurred a few years ago: A ship was coming back from the other side of the sea, and on it were a great many people, and one day the passengers sang that glorious song, "Jesus, Lover of My Soul." As they sang it, one of the singers was strangely attracted by a voice just behind him, and he looked around and searched the face of the singer. When the song was finished, the stranger introduced himself to the one whose voice so strikingly arrested his attention, and said, "Were you in the Civil War in the sixties?" He said, "I was; I was a Confederate soldier." "I thought you were," replied the first; "it all comes back to me; you were one night on picket duty and hummed the song we have just sung. I was a Union soldier, in command of a squad of men. That night we heard you sing this same song. Tenderly you sang the words:

> All my trust on Thee is stayed;
> All my help from Thee I bring;
> Cover my defenseless head
> With the shadow of Thy wing!

"We had our guns leveled on you, but when you came to those words I said, 'Boys, we must not shoot such a man as that!'" And now, after those many years, they thus met. How do you explain that deliverance? God touched the hearts of those Union soldiers and held back their will and their bullets from this poor man's head. It is no wonder that the soldier from the South and from the North there on the ship went into each other's arms and blessed God for the overruling providence of the One who never slumbers nor sleeps, and who never forgets to care for His own. Oh, if men would be wise in their relations to God! If He be left out of their plans, then are they doomed.

An eminent Texas lawyer told me recently an incident confirmatory of the very lesson I am now mentioning. Twenty-five years ago when this lawyer came to make his home in the city where he yet resides, he and the richest man in the city saw a great deal of each other. The rich man disregarded God; he caroused, he reveled, he went to the bad. He lived only for this world. The Christian lawyer said, "One evening I was going up the street to the church to prayer-meeting, and I met this man, and he said: 'Where are you going?' calling me by name. I said, 'I am going to prayer-meeting. You had better go with me.' He said, 'Prayer-meeting, and you a practical lawyer! You ought to have more sense than that. You will not get any cases at that rate. Nobody will want you for their lawyer. People don't want prayer-meeting men for lawyers. You had better come with me and go to the dram shop and let us have a good time together.'" Said the lawyer, "I made an earnest plea that the end of that way was death. He laughed me to scorn. But only a few years passed, only a few, until all his property was gone, the property of that God-forgetting man. All his property was gone, and his household wrecked and his prospects blasted, and he died a pauper and was buried by the county." O men, my brothers, there is a vital difference between God's man and the man not His.

I have spoken long enough. You will indulge me another word. Our constant danger is that we shall look too largely at material things. We must see Him who is invisible, and trust in Him and in His love. We are at times greatly cast down. We must look up. That is our hope. The text is true. They that be for us are infinitely more than they that be against us. Sometimes we see justice perverted. Sometimes we see the ends of righteousness caricatured. Sometimes court-house trials are a contemptible farce. Sometimes the saddest spectacles of the miscarriage of law openly and defiantly blaze in a city's life. You will be cast down by many things if you take short views and look merely at earthly things. God reigns and cares and loves. They that be for us are infinitely more than they that be against us. Look up, my brethren, look up. And at the last, know that the day does come when every weapon against God shall be ground to the finest powder. Job's question is the question that sounds through the ages: "Who hath hardened himself against Him and hath prospered?" Never one. The prosperity may seem to be there, but it is only the crackling of the dry thorns consumed by the fire. There is no prosperity for a living creature that lives in permanent defiance of the will and Word of Almighty God. At the end of such defiance there are the ashes of remorse and the doom of death. Men and women who hear me today, what are your real relations to God? Have you made peace with Him? Are you right with Him? Do you see God, as did Elisha? Do you reckon upon His infinite power? Are you in harmony with His will? Is your vision of eternal things keen and clear? Do you walk by faith and not by sight? Are God's purposes real and are His promises personal to you? In the secrecy and deepest sincerity of your souls, I pray you today, each one for himself, to lay these questions to heart. Do take time to realize God.

11
The Supreme Gift to Jesus

As we come to this first Lord's Day of the New Year, the one sentence that has kept ringing in my heart as a suitable word for us today is the oft quoted saying of Paul concerning the Macedonian Christians, namely:

But first gave their own selves to the Lord (2 Cor. 8:5).

Paul is here praising the early Macedonian Christians in words remarkably gracious and heartening, as you observed while you listened to the scriptural reading, a moment ago, from the eighth chapter of Second Corinthians. Praise from Paul was certainly noteworthy. He was no fulsome flatterer. He spoke words straight and direct and true. When men needed rebuking, Paul was just the man to give such rebuke. And now, when he finds an unusual case of devotion to Christ, and of sacrifice for Christ, and of glorious witnessing to the power of the grace of Christ, Paul sets it forth in this chapter in words that fairly breathe with beauty and blessing.

These early Macedonian Christians, though sorely afflicted themselves, with their means of living pitifully reduced, yet out of their affliction and poverty got together an offering for some needy people far away. Though themselves in dire distress, yet with all the good will of the givers, and with a prayer for God's favor upon their united gifts, they sent their offerings, voluntarily and joyfully, to far-away people who were in need. Paul makes a telling discourse upon such an unusual deed, and pays his tribute to it in a way that makes life loom larger and the possibilities of human nature seem grander as we read his tribute.

But the point of his praise is what we need to see clearly today; and that is that no man can please Christ and do His will as He wishes until the supreme thing is done toward Christ and for Him, namely, until life itself is unreservedly laid on the altar for Him. When one's life is fully laid on the altar for Christ, all else in service for Him is easy and natural and blessed, because the greater includes the less. Just as long as a Christian proposes to serve God with little driblets of money and time and service, the Christian life is vitiated and stunted and misrepresented. But when a Christian faithfully apprehends the truth that the Christian life calls for the actual giving of life unto Him who gave His life for us, then a thousand smaller questions are settled in one moment, and settled once for all.

There are two simple but practically vital truths that may be seen in this story of the Macedonian Christians, whose conduct called forth such positive praise from Paul.

First of all, these early Christians put the cause of Christ as the first thing in their lives. Wasn't that altogether praiseworthy and consistent and necessary? Where should Christ's cause be put? I am speaking this morning to an army of Christian men and women, and upon you, one by one, I would press the question, even as with a sword point, upon the deepest conscience. Where should Christ's cause be put by the friends of Christ? These early Christians clearly put it as the first thing in their lives. Untold mischief comes to Christian men and women, and to the vital cause that they represent, when they higgle and haggle and fail to put Christ's cause as the first thing in their lives, making it the center and heart of their thought and activity.

The most superficial views are often taken by Christians concerning the Christian life. It is sometimes vainly thought that if we can add largely to our numbers, then are we indeed making progress. It does not necessarily follow that an army is making progress because it keeps adding soldiers to the ranks. The Bible never one time gives any such hint that an increase in numbers is the way of progress in the Christian warfare. The Bible never once gives any encouragement to the doctrine that we shall be strong according to our numbers. Indeed, we are warned again and again, by warnings direct and implied, as to the snare that there is in numbers. There stands out like some dark cloud in old story of David's numbering the kingdoms of Israel and Judah, to warn God's people forever that they must not put their confidence in numbers. Never once does God put the emphasis on numbers. Read the story of Gideon's vast army reduced to three hundred men, and see how God utterly discounts numbers. Often it is given us to see how God signalizes the mighty victories that may be obtained by handfuls, consecrated and definitely committed to His program. It is not "How many do we count in the kingdom of God?" but "How much do we weigh?" It is not quantity in the kingdom of God that counts, but it is quality. You can sometimes put your hand on one man in a community who seems to have the power of a thousand ordinary Christian men. His very nod is empire; his very footfall law; the very crook of his finger is power. The explanation is that he lives his religion. It is not duration that counts in human life, but intensity. Some men die at thirty and have done more for humanity than others dying at one hundred and thirty. The first mentioned live while they live, with the one motive of doing the will of God.

Again, it is manifest that men sometimes have the mistaken conception that if they had more money they could forward Christ's cause in a victorious way. They were never more mistaken. Never one time is the emphasis in the Bible put upon material, visible resources. To be sure, I have no sympathy at all with the anarchistic outcry that is sometimes heard against money. I do not hesitate to say that men who can make money ought to make it—legitimately, to be sure—for all illegitimately gained money is a curse to him who gains it. Men who have gifts in the world of business, commanding gifts, strategic gifts, who can amass money legitimately and properly, ought to do so; but money in the kingdom of God is not the supreme thing at all. The early disciples of Jesus were without money, and yet they shook the Roman empire to its foundations with their spiritual power. They did not have vast bank accounts, and yet the pagan empire was shot through with gleams of heavenly light in one short generation. Money is not the supreme thing in the kingdom of God. Full many a time it is a terrible handicap, a perilous hindrance. Full many a time men turn to it instead of to the arm invisible and almighty. To the degree that men put their confidence in human, visible, material resources, to that degree are they weak and not strong at all.

What then is the supreme thing to be laid to heart in the kingdom of God? It is pointed out here for us by these Macedonian Christians. It is to put Christ's cause as the first thing in our thinking and doing, literally to put it first, and to build around it as the center of all our thought and all our activity. These early Christians, by the glorious example described here for us by Paul, point the way for us, if we would make the Christian life a thing of ever-growing happiness and ever-increasing triumph over the world about us. How all things would be changed about us if we would put First things First!

Now, Christ's cause is to be put first by Christians—not off in a corner, treated as some little stepchild, unloved and in the way. Christ's cause is to be put first everywhere, and forever to be put first. That is the need of the world today. The one constant tug at my heart concerning this pan-European war is that it will blazon forth the truth before all the nations that the one kingdom that is to have supreme attention at the hands of humanity, because it is the one hope of humanity, is the kingdom of Christ. The only kingdom that shall last, the one kingdom that shall ultimately break to pieces every other kingdom, the one kingdom whose right it is to have undisputed sway in all the earth, is Christ's kingdom, and Christ's friends should always and everywhere put His kingdom first. That is the outstanding need of the world today. "Seek ye first the kingdom of God and His righteousness." Seek it first—not secondly, nor thirdly, nor subordinately, nor optionally, nor incidentally. "Put My cause first" is ever the call of Jesus to His people. Put it first when you go to the bank. Put it first when you stand before court and jury. Put it first when you go from house to house ministering to the sick. Put it first when you stand in the high place of the teacher. Put it first in the pulpit. Put it first in the market-place. Put it first in the realm of government. "Put My kingdom, My cause, My will, first," is forever His call. One is King and Lawgiver for humanity, and that is Christ. Christians are to hear this call, and act on it, and live it, and relate all life to it. That is what the world supremely needs. It is not fine church houses; it is not buildings marked with marvelous architecture; it is not delicately stained glass windows; it is not eloquent preachers; it is not vast piles of money; it is not large numbers. Its need is for men and women who are themselves separated unto Christ and whose dominant concern is to put His will first. Such men and women are to be the salt of the earth, to put their healing touch on the whole mass of needy and unredeemed humanity. That is the world's first need—to put Christ first.

Paul stated it for us when he said, "To me to live is Christ"; or, freely translated, "To me to live is for Christ to live over again." Said Paul: "I am to think His thoughts, and to talk His talk, and to do His deeds as best I can, and to live His life, and to offer myself as did He for humanity." That is the business of a Christian in this world. What other business could a Christian have? After I am redeemed from the curse of the law, by Jesus, who died for me, the Just for the unjust, the Sinless for the sinner, I am left for a little while in the earth to reincarnate the spirit, the teaching, the life, of Jesus, and I am to put Him first. So that, when Paul said: "Ye are not your own; ye are bought with a price. Therefore, glorify God in your body and in your spirit, which are His," he was just stating the simplest, plainest, fairest truth that can be put into human words. You Christian men and women literally belong to Christ. I charge you therefore to put His cause where it ought to be. Let His will be regnant in all human life just as it ought to be. Then even this earthly life is, indeed, a thing of surpassing glory.

You will observe that these early Macedonian Christians, in all their various callings, thus enthroned Christ's will and made it regnant in all their daily temporal affairs. The religion of the Lord Jesus Christ is not simply a showy business for Sunday. If you are going to make any choice, and put your best foot forward at some particular time, in Christian living, do it yonder in the market-place, rather than here when you are singing some beautiful hymn. Do it in the home, where the nervous, impatient child is taxing you to the limit. Live for Christ out there, where you closely touch humanity, where all the sharp currents of life clash. There put the will of Christ first. These early Christians in all their daily avocations put Christ's cause first. Oh, isn't that what we need, what we supremely need? We are going to get on miserably if a man is a schemer and a cheat yonder in his business, and a pious, long-faced saint here in church. We are going to get on badly if the teacher forgets and is a nervous scold in the schoolhouse, where plastic life is being touched and shaped by her every minute. What the world needs is for this leaven of Christianity to be incarnated in our lives, as we touch humanity the six busy days in the week, as well as on the Lord's Day. The grocery man ought to be better, and the laundry man, and the messenger boy, and the butcher, and the telegraph boy, and the doctor, and all the rest, because you and I cross their paths, and look into their faces, and greet them for a moment in life's daily battle. Our Christianity is to be radiant out there in the midst of the seething humanity which is dying without God. It was so with these early Christians, because they put Christ's cause first.

What a glorious day that will be—may God speed its full triumph—when in all callings and among all classes and conditions of humanity shall be realized that noble injunction of Paul: "Whether ye eat or drink, or whatsoever ye do, do all to the glory of God." I can see how the modest teacher, just as truly as any prophet in his pulpit, can glorify God at her far-reaching task. I can see how the lawyer, standing before court and jury, can mightily glorify God, as he pleads for the fundamental principles of righteousness and justice and mercy. I can see how the financier, and the struggling girl with her typewriter, and the needlewoman, the farmer, the man driving the dray—humanity in all its phases and at all its tasks out there in the big battle of life—can glorify God as really as did Paul, if each one will simply put Christ's cause where the Macedonian Christians put it—put it first.

Isn't it a glorious thing that we have the examples in this dear country of ours of many of our clearest-minded and most influential men who put Christ first? Whatever may be your politics, that does not concern me at all; that never concerns the pulpit. The preacher is as much concerned for the souls of men who follow one political party as another. But whatever may be your politics, you must be profoundly grateful for Woodrow Wilson, that modest but mighty Christian man at the helm of this nation; and you must be likewise grateful for the Secretary of State, Mr. Bryan; and you must be deeply grateful for that masterful leader yonder in Great Britain, Lloyd George—grateful that these personalities, world-touching personalities, bow down like little children, daily asking for wisdom and strength from God for their tasks. The gracious influence of such men for Christianity is literally beyond human computation. And here in your own modest circles of life there are men in this task, and women in that, who are incarnating the ideals of Jesus, and are putting His cause first, and they in their sphere, are positively and constantly blessing humanity. God speed the day when Christians, when you and I here in this meeting-house this first Lord's Day morning of the New Year, shall understand that what Christ waits for and asks at our hands is that we will do in life what we are here to do! That we will have the right sense of our vocation! And that we will relate ourselves to the one embracing task that we are in the world for, here in the little vestibule of time preceding eternity, to put Christ's cause first, and then pass from time to be with Him in the larger House of Life, where all the conditions of life are perfect forevermore!

There is another vital truth to be emphasized, and that is that the secret of such wonderful devotion on the part of these Macedonian Christians is explained in the very words of the brief text:

"But first they gave their own selves to the Lord." As certainly as we are here, my brothers, the crux of the whole matter of living the Christian life is stated here in this sentence: "But first they gave their own selves to the Lord." You have a thousand questions settled when this one big question is settled: I am here to go where, and to speak what, and to live as, Christ wishes, and to that I dedicate my life. When that is done, the many questions of life all adjust themselves into harmonious concord with the one consuming purpose of life.

Note carefully the words: "But first they gave their own selves to the Lord." They gave themselves. It is just at that point that we most sadly fail as Christians. We propose to give Jesus little compartments in our lives, and then desire Him to leave us to ourselves with the larger compartments. Oh, that is the tragedy of our Christianity! These early Christians just did what a Christian is in the world for, what you and I are here for—namely, to do Christ's will, to represent Christ, to be His witness, to be His friend, to carry forward His kingdom, to make victorious His will everywhere. If we can carry out His will by ill health better than by good health, let ill health come! If we can do it better by poverty than by riches, let us have poverty! If we can do it better to be persecuted and hunted and sent to our graves misunderstood, Lord, let it be that way! Thy will be enthroned and made victorious through us, come as it will, cost what it may! It is not a theory that you and I are inescapably responsible for the doing of the will of God. That is the preeminent fact of life.

I have told you before of scenes I have witnessed and lessons I have learned in connection with the camp-meetings I have attended with the cattlemen, here and there, in the great West. It is one of the most refreshing joys of my life thus to be with them. They are heroes and empire builders. One morning I preached to that great group of cattlemen, gathered in a cleft of the mountains, perhaps a thousand men, on this searching text: "Ye are bought with a price; therefore, glorify God in your body, and in your spirit, which are God's." And that morning I was making the insistence that Christ should be the absolute Master of life, just as I am making it this morning. When the service was done, one of those cattlemen locked his arm in mine and said, "If you are willing, we will go for a walk. I have something to say to you."

And up the long mountain canyon we took our walk, more than a mile away from the many camps. He said not a word as we were going. His great chest rose and fell like some seething furnace. It was evident that he had something serious to say, and I waited from him to break the silence. When we were more than a mile away, he turned and faced me, and with gasping words he said, "I want you to pray a dedicatory prayer for me." I said, "What do you wish to dedicate?" And then he said with sobs, "I never knew until today that I am responsible for my very property to Jesus; I have not been a Christian long, and I have not heard much about Him, and I do not know much about what He expects of me. I never knew until you preached today that all these thousands of cattle, every hoof of them, that I have said were mine, are not really mine, but that they belong to Christ, and that I am simply His administrator, His trustee, His steward. Never until today did I know that. And I never knew until today that these twenty-five miles and more of spreading ranch lands, that I have said were mine, are not mine at all, but His; that the title to every acre is in Him; not until today did I know that. Now," he said, "I want you to bow down here and tell Him for me that I will take my place; I will accept my stewardship; I will be His administrator on His estate.

And then when you are through, I wish to pray." Of course I prayed the best I could, the man consenting and assenting, with sobs and words, as I prayed. And when I had finished and waited for him to pray, he waited some minutes before he could speak, sobbing like a little child; and when, at last, he did speak, he said, "Master, am I not in a position now to give you also the loved one for whom I have long been praying? Am I not in a position now to give him to you? Along with all else, I do give him to you; save him for your glory; I give him to you today forever." We walked back to the camp, and not a word was said on the return journey.

Then the day wore to evening, and the men again came to-gether for worship, and I stood before them in that mountain canyon, once more to preach. Nor had I preached a dozen minutes until the wild young fellow on the outskirts of the great crowd of a thousand cowmen rose up and said, "I cannot wait until that man is done his sermon to tell you that I have found the Lord!" Do you doubt that there was a vital and fundamental connection between the right relation of that ranchman to Jesus Christ and the home-coming of him for whom he prayed? Oh, there is no telling, my brothers, how much power a man may have to drive back Satan and beat down the very mountains of sin; there is no telling how much helpful power any man or woman may have, would have, even you and I, if only we will relate ourselves to the will of Christ like we ought. These early Christians did that, and the glory of God was over them beyond all words to tell.

You will notice that they did it voluntarily. Paul said, "They were willing of themselves." Nobody coerced them. Nobody drove them. Nobody scolded them. Nobody sought to wheedle money out of them by all sorts of vain pleas. God pity us! I have no respect for that sort of thing in religion. Here these men came, and they laid themselves, their very lives, on the altar, for Christ. When a man does that supreme thing for Christ, is there any problem in his giving? Is there any problem in his giving money or time or talk or service? When the supreme thing has been given to Christ, you have gone to the heart of the Christian life; and then the Christian life can be made a great sun, lighting up the darkness near and far, and piloting many in the upward way.

Here is the test and here is the measure of our power to bless humanity. I tell you, no matter how brilliant a man is, no matter how gifted, no matter how generous, if he will not put his life into the service of Christ, he shall come short utterly of the supreme thing. Life must be given for life. Life must make its impact on life. Far more than all the checks you can ever write is the writing of yourself into the right kind of service for a weary, sinful humanity. Incomparably better than any check that you will ever lay on the altar of Christ is for you to lay yourself on Christ's altar. You have bewailed the fact that you did not have the money to give. You forget that you have something so much better than money. You have bewailed the fact that you lived from hand to mouth and could not put your dollars and hundreds on the altar for Jesus, as do others; but you could put something on the altar for Christ in comparison with which money seems but as a trifle. "I seek not yours, but you." That means that Christ seeks your manhood, your womanhood, your personality, your individuality, your reputation, your character, your tongue, your brain, your example, your very life. Humanity waits for that, and the kingdom of God comes—comes with power, comes to conquer, when Christian men and women put themselves, their lives, on the altar for their King and Redeemer.

That is the lesson for us today. That is the supreme lesson out of this old-time story. O preacher, and there are numbers here today, and be assured that your coming always makes us glad, you and I shall make pitiful progress in our exalted calling if we do not die to self and live to Christ! O Sunday school worker, you will make slow progress if you have imagined you have discharged your Christian task when you have sat before your class once a week, for forty-five minutes or less, and have said a few things about the lesson. There are no secularities in the right kind of a Christian life. You and I are to put ourselves on Christ's altar twenty-four hours a day, living for Christ, sleeping when we sleep to His glory, serving or resting or eating or suffering or going or waiting, all for Christ. Whatever He wishes, that is the supreme lesson we are to learn and to translate into daily deed.

Have you thus given yourself to Christ? O my friends, what is your spiritual condition today? Are you halting Christians, derelict Christians, duty-neglecting Christians, backslidden Christians, with your years hurrying like the flying clouds? Are you to go on like that until, some evening when the shadows of the night come to shroud the world, you come down to sudden death and startle your family with the gasp: "I have lived with practically no thought of Christ at all"? O men and women, the one thing that makes life really great is that we are here for a little season to do the Father's will, just like Jesus who came down from heaven, saying, "My meat is to do the will of Him that sent me, and to finish His work." Is that your thought of life, your effort in life? Are you related to Christ

today like you ought to be? We ought willingly to go through fire
and flood to do anything Christ wishes at our hands, when we remember what He did and does for us. He gave His all for me. Yon
cross was for me. That bloody sweat in Gethsemane, O God, was for
me. That cry after cry, while the world was darkened, and the earth
was shaking, and the sun would not shine on that scene of scenes,
all that was for me. O soul, is gratitude dead within thee? O man,
hast thou lost all sense of the eternal proprieties? After what Christ
did for us, surely we are ready to go any length for Him. Don't you
say so today? With all my heart I would say it for myself. If this is
to be my last year, O our God, I would dedicate myself to make it
better than any previous year, to help more people, to gladden and
bless more lives, to hearten souls, God helping me! O men and
women, let us put Christ first. Let us seek to bury all our pitiful mistakes, wanderings and defects in one great heap today, and let us say,
"Master, from today Thou shalt be first with me and mine!" Oh, the
happiness in such a life as that! Oh, the safety of such a life as that!
Oh, the usefulness of such a life, for that is the life planted like a tree
by the rivers of water, in the glorious service of Christ.

Are there those here today who say: "Sir, we never did begin the
Christian life at all?" Then, I ask, don't you think it is high time that
you awake out of sleep? The day is far spent. Opportunity is passing, even now. Don't you think it is time today to be rightly related
to Jesus? We are going to sing one of the most beautiful hymns that
is ever sung, and while we sing it I wonder if there are not duty-
neglecting Christians present who will say, "Without waiting to
confer with flesh or blood, today I renew my vows with God, I do
my duty today. Down in my deepest conscience I hear a voice, a cla-
mant voice, a voice calling me to active service in Christ's church;
I will obey today." Come then to these front pews and wait. There
are others who say, "We cannot take that step, we are not ready to
go that far; but we do wish today to take the great step of the public commitment of ourselves to Christ, who alone forgiveth and
saveth sinners. We will receive Him as our Savior and yield our lives
to His control this Lord's Day morning, the first of the New Year,
that Christ may forgive and cleanse and save and guard and guide

and use us from this day forward and forever, according to His holy will." You, too, come, while now we sing, and before all the people let the great confession be made of your choice of the Lord Jesus Christ as your Savior and Master today and forevermore.

12

The Subject and the Object of the Gospel

(Annual Sermon preached before the Southern Baptist Convention at Louisville, Ky., May 12, 1899.)

Unto me, who am less than the least of all saints, is this grace given, that I should preach among the Gentiles the unsearchable riches of Christ (Eph. 3:8).

First and foremost of all Christ's servants in the work and triumphs of Christianity stands the apostle Paul. And yet the most marked characteristic of his wondrous life was his humility. If any man might have presumed to profess "sinless perfection," Paul was that man; but he would have regarded such profession as an unspeakable blasphemy. See how he speaks of himself: "Unto me who am less than the least of all saints." A few years before he designates himself as "the least of the apostles." And just a few years later he confesses that he is the "chief of sinners." As he grew in the experimental knowledge of God's grace, he also grew in humility and self-distrust. Humility always obtains in proportion as men see the goodness and greatness of God. It was so with Job and Jeremiah, and Isaiah. It is ever so.

These men who do not know whether Christ is much, are certain to think themselves much. Those whom God greatly honors in service are those whom He first greatly humbles.

"God resisteth the proud and giveth grace to the humble." And when He gives grace to the humble He gives all other grace. "Only by pride cometh contention." Pride was the chief ingredient in the sin that turned angels into demons. If Satan ever again knows what it is to hope, it surely must be when he sees Christ's preacher inflated with his own proud conceit, for he remembers that this was the snare whereby he fell into eternal condemnation.

Well pleased is our great Master when He sees the becoming grace of humility adorning the lives of His servants. Both by precept and example He magnified its beauty and power. His whole earthly life was the illustration and demonstration of His saying, "I am among you as one that serveth." And constant was His reiteration of the great truth, "Whosoever would be first among you let him be servant of all." The true motto for all His people is that spoken by John: "He must increase, but I must decrease."

Notwithstanding the lowly view Paul had of himself, he greatly magnified God's grace in making him a preacher of the gospel. Everywhere Paul went, his life bore out the saying, "I magnify mine office." The preacher who does not should at once give up his office.

Nothing can take the place of the Christian ministry. The progress of civilization, the making of many books, the increase of schools and learning, the marvelous triumphs of the press—mighty as are all of these agencies—they can never supersede the divinely sent preacher. "It pleased God by the foolishness of preaching to save them that believe."

Let not Christ's minister for one moment lose sight of the divineness of his mission. Of such preacher some one has truly said, "He holds a divine commission, he proclaims a divine revelation, he is animated by a divine purpose, he accomplishes a divine result, he is dependent upon a divine Spirit." If the preacher will but be true to his sublime and divine appointment, he shall stand among men without rivalry or competition—earth's mightiest man. In the great crises of the past, matchless has been the influence wielded by God's prophets and preachers. When all other voices have failed, they have rallied the wavering people to the standards of truth and righteousness.

It was the golden-mouthed Chrysostom who became the oracle of the hour in the days when Antioch was smitten with terror. It was the flaming Augustine who rallied his fellow countrymen from despair and breathed into their lives new hope and purpose, when imperial Rome lay bleeding and trampled beneath the heel of an invading oppressor. It was the plain, yet invincible Luther, who, when reeking corruption reigned in the papal court and spread its blight over all Europe, spoke forth words that echoed as the thunder and were piercing as the lightning, stirring a revolution that thrilled all Christendom and marking a new epoch in the civilization of the world.

As in the past, so shall it be in the future, that God's foremost instrument is His preacher, in both the civilization and the evangelization of the world.

Let it also be said in passing that there was an element in Paul's preaching that must needs be in all effective preaching. It was his tone of authority. He believed with all his heart his message, and as God's ambassador he delivered it without quailing, for one moment, under any fire. "There's untold power in him who knows his mission is a thing of God's own willing, and that it cannot fail, though doubts may shroud in cloud the transient hour." It is conviction that convinces. Earth's last place for stammering and indefiniteness is the pulpit. Christ's ambassador is to proclaim his Master's message rather than to defend it. He is a witness rather than an advocate. Christianity is nothing if it is not dogmatic. It has no reason for its existence if it is not sublimely positive. It is not a conundrum to be guessed at, or a theory to be speculated upon, but it is a divine revelation which is to be implicitly accepted and followed with the deepest heartthrob of our lives. Christ's preacher is not here primarily to teach Christian evidences or apologetics, but his message is like that of the prophet of old—"Thus saith the Lord."

To be continually on the defensive is contrary to the very genius and purpose of the gospel. The preacher is to be concerned mainly with the preaching of positive truth rather than the refutation of passing error. Let not the last blatant attack of infidelity against the Bible be noticed overmuch. It is not the chief business of God's minister to answer the last fool who has escaped from the mortar in which he was brayed. The gospel faithfully preached is its own best defense. Let us who preach remember that we speak by divine authority; not theories, but facts; not what we don't know, but what our souls do know to their profoundest depths. I give it as the humble but deepest conviction of my heart that the overmastering necessity of the modern pulpit is a return to that dogmatic tone of authority that characterized the apostles in the preaching of the gospel, and that must be found in all effective preaching the world over. O my brethren, if we shall but magnify our office as did Paul and be content just to be faithful preachers of Christ, blessed, eternally blessed, shall be the results of our ministry.

> 'Tis not a cause of small import,
> A preacher's care demands;
> But what might fill an angel's heart,
> And filled the Savior's hands.

Paul was saved for a specific purpose—he was called unto a great mission. It is so with all the redeemed of Christ. What was Paul's mission? He tells us in our text: "That I should preach among the Gentiles the unsearchable riches of Christ." Let two thoughts growing out of the text engage our attention.

First. The subject-matter of the preacher's message.

Second. The ministry is the heaven-appointed exponent of the mission of every redeemed soul.

The first thought of our text is the following:

I. The subject-matter of the preacher's message. From the day when Paul first stood up as a witness for Christianity, until that eventful day when he laid his head upon the block as a martyr for the truth, he unwaveringly held to one great theme, and that theme was salvation through the blood of Jesus Christ. Once in his long ministry he seemed somewhat to leave his theme. It was when he contended with the philosophers of Athens in his oration on Mars Hill. And there, beyond all other places, did his labors prove most feeble. It is significant that immediately afterwards when he came to Corinth he "determined not to know anything among them, save Jesus Christ and Him crucified." Always and everywhere he is careful thus to go on record: "We preach not ourselves but Christ Jesus the Lord." The heaven-appointed center for all true preaching is Jesus Christ, and to leave that center is to lose the dominant power and purpose of the gospel.

The plan of human redemption, with Christ as the great keystone in the mystic arch, is the culmination and perfection of God's infinite mercy, wisdom and love. To bring it to the attention of man, to vitalize it and make it a reality to him, all the providences of God have been directed for 6,000 years. From the hour that the smoking blood of man's first offering rose from the sacrificial altar down through the ages to the tragedy of Calvary, every act of worship, every command of God, and every providence were so many sign-boards pointing to that last and supreme act in God's wonderful plan. Calvary has been the focal point upon which all the powers of darkness have hurled their darts, and it has been the glorious prism that has caught the light of heaven and sent its refracted rays into the thick darkness of earth. To make a world, to create a system, to swing into space this mighty canvas, was the work of a word.

But the plan of man's redemption required the highest effort of the divine mind. It vacated the throne of the Son in heaven and brought the "mighty God" to earth to dwell among men. In the fullness of time, God sent Him forth and yonder He lies the infant of Mary in Bethlehem's manger. For thirty and three years He walks the earthly way "a Man of sorrows and acquainted with grief." "He is despised and rejected of men." They plot for His destruction. The last night of His life has come and He is betrayed into the hands of His enemies. A mock trial is hurriedly had, and He is adjudged to die upon the cruel cross. The awful hour for His death has come and hellish malice nails Him to the shameful tree. Between heaven and earth He hangs, suffering, bleeding, praying, dying. His head has fallen upon His breast. He is dead. They take Him down and now earth's darkest night has come—the Lord of life and glory lies silent in the grave. The fiends of darkness now rise up and hope begins to bloom in hell, for the Sun of Righteousness has been eclipsed! Ah, wait! Sing not too fast, ye legions of the pit! The dark night will pass away and there will dawn a victorious morning. The morning has dawned. The fallen Conqueror breaks the bands of death and puts the grave beneath His feet. Before a gazing world He ascends on high, leading captivity captive, and gives gifts to men. And now again He is on His throne, where He reigns and loves and waits, to give salvation to any one who will only dare to trust Him.

My brethren in the ministry, if Christ has given unto us the grace of preaching, though like Moses we may have but a stammering tongue, yet in view of what man's redemption cost, in view of its divine authority and purpose, shall we ever in any presence, under any earthly pressure, for any kind of reason so far forget our heaven-appointed mission, so grieve our dear Redeemer, so wrong a dying world, as to preach anything else except the riches of the Lord Jesus Christ? Preach philosophy, or science, or culture, or worldly wisdom, or beautiful platitudes, preach merely to please men or entertain? Sooner far let us commend to the lips of a famishing child a painted glass filled with painted water; or to a starving castaway apples of Sodom; or to a heartbroken mother a poem on the North Pole; or to a dying sinner the fables of Aesop.

Here, brethren, is our message made out for us. It is Jesus Christ—in His divine personality, in the spotlessness of His humanity, in His offices as Prophet, Priest and King, in the atoning efficacy of His death, in the power of His resurrection, in the prevalence of His intercession, in the certainty and purpose of His coming again.

Does someone venture to say that this theme is "too narrow"? Before he does, let him remember that "the foolishness of God is wiser than man, and the weakness of God is stronger than men." Let him remember also that Christ on the cross is the harmony of every doctrine of divine revelation. There is seen the enormity of man's sin and its infinite punishment. There the mercy and truth of God meet together, and there His justice and love are made to shine with eternal glory. This theme "too narrow?" It is an infinite ocean ever expanding before Him who seeks to know its meaning. Well does Paul say of it that it is "unsearchable." In Christ is seen the procuring cause of man's justification, redemption, sanctification and glorification forever with God. In Him is infinite knowledge for every student, and comfort for all broken-heartedness, and forgiveness for every penitent wanderer. This is the only balm in Gilead that will surely heal the health of earth's sorrowing, sin-sick people. We "daub with untempered mortar" when we dare to preach anything else for the healing of the sorrow and sin of a ruined world. Man's sinfulness is ever the same, and Christ's gospel is ever the same, and this message alone will break up the fallow ground of a sinful heart and turn it to God. Wherever it has gone, from king to barbarian, it has turned men from darkness to light and from the power of Satan unto God.

Why should we preach Christ and Him only? Because this is the "only name under heaven given among men whereby we must be saved," and it is to save souls that we are called into Christ's service. Every other duty of the preacher is incidental to this one supreme and all-controlling object of the gospel. Yet all the preachers in the world left to themselves could not bring to repentance one child of sin. Christ must save and Christ alone. He left us the supreme lesson in homiletics when He said, "And I, if I be lifted up from the earth, will draw all men unto Me." It is the attractive power of the cross, gleaming like a searchlight through the words and thoughts of the preacher, that kindles a fire on the altar of the sinner's conscience, and turns him to God. It is only of Christ that the divine Spirit testifies, and utterly futile, "twice dead, plucked up by the roots," are all our efforts, if we do not have the Holy Spirit's fructifying presence and power.

Paul knew whence came his power. He knew that with all his strength of wisdom and learning, left to himself, he was as powerless to save a soul as an atom floating in the sunbeam is to quench the sun. Salvation by any human merit was to him a criminal doctrine. He preached salvation by the Lord. In every message he boldly avowed the deity of Jesus of Nazareth, in whom dwelled all the fullness of the Godhead bodily. He was God manifest in the flesh, God over all, with unquestioned and absolute right to the loyalty and love of every human heart. Christianity does not ask for compliments. Christ is all and in all. We are not of those who believe in a Congress of Religions where Christ may receive little if any larger attention than Brahma, or Buddha, or Mohammed, or Joseph Smith; or where it may even be conceded that Christianity is the best form of religion, provided it be also understood that all the other religions contain essential and saving truths. No, with all our souls we will denounce such treason against Jesus Christ. Christ is God, or He is the arch-deceiver of the ages. And for every theory against His deity, whether it be Socinian, Sabellian, Unitarian, or what not, we will say to their advocates: "Gentlemen, your theories are unutterably contemptible to us, and we will have none of your bouquets about Christ's 'splendid humanity' while you scout His deity." But our challenge shall be this: "If the Lord be God, follow Him; but if Baal, then follow him."

We should preach Christ and Christ only, because we have no warrant or authority for preaching anything else. Paul wrote to the Galatians: "But though we, or an angel from heaven, preach any other gospel unto you than that which we have preached unto you, let him be accursed." And then in the very next breath, in order more deeply to impress this fundamental truth with the curse attendant upon its violation, he repeats the awful sentence: "As we said before, so say I know again, if any man preach any other gospel unto you than that ye have received, let him be accursed." Ah, brethren, like Paul, we will have no "other gospel," for if salvation through the atonement of Christ shall fail, then all has failed, for this is the very ultimatum of God.

To be sure "other gospels" are abroad these latter days, but we shall unwaveringly hold to the one—"Christ and Him crucified." And though many are seeking to be rid of that word "crucified," to us the great central fact of our redemption is that "Christ bore our sins in His own body on the tree." Salvation by His blood shall ever be our theme—we will know no other. We are not ignorant of the "other gospels" that are now being offered as substitutes for the one. We have the gospel of philosophy, the gospel of culture, the gospel of science, the gospel of sociology, the gospel of refined humanitarianism that is stealthily finding its way into some pulpits and is gilding much of our modern literature as it softly talks about "reconstructed manhood." We know about them all, and we know that with all their keenness of speculation and polish of learning and profundity of philosophy, not one of them has ever regenerated a single soul. We are not of those who have concluded that the old gospel of the cross is unsuited to the advanced thought and aesthetic taste of these cultured times. Not philosophy, nor culture, nor sociology, nor humanitarianism, in fullest possible measure, can save lost men. Underneath them all, the human heart will still sin on and sigh for Emanuel's peace and pardon. The old, old story uttered by lips touched by a live coal from off God's altar and driven home to men's consciences with the voice of divine authority—this and this only can make the spiritual wilderness to blossom as the rose. It was such preaching by George Whitefield that, more than all things else, stirred the heart of the calculating Franklin, and sent terror to the soul of the skeptical Hume. This was the theme of Spurgeon for nearly forty years, and under his ministry, more than any other in his generation, lost men came flocking to God as doves to their windows, and great Christian enterprises sprang up like magic, and the ever-increasing philanthropy and spiritual power of his church has been the wonder of this century.

In contrast with such preaching, shall I say a word about the trivial and sensational themes of some modern pulpits? Many of them make us blush for very shame, for they are a travesty upon the high calling of Christ's ambassador. Take this series of sermons for instance—mind you, of *sermons:* Shakespeare, Business, Courting, The Scolding Wife, The Husband Who Stays Out Late at Night, The Bicycle, The Two-headed Woman, Jack and the Beanstalk, Tan Shoes and Negligee Shirts, Did Man Come from the Monkey? Ah, when the preacher will thus pose as a mountebank and turn the sanctuary of God into a show house, do you wonder at Sidney

Smith's saying? It was this: "There are three orders in creation, men, women, and preachers." All such sensationalism in the pulpit is worse than sawdust. It is born of the secular and smacks of the street, and is a burning shame upon the Christian ministry. If the history of preaching proves anything, it proves that the preacher can have no deep and permanent grasp of power except as he holds up Christ and the great doctrines inseparable from Him. No other preaching will even secure lasting morality, not to speak of regeneration.

Surely if any man who ever lived might have hoped for good results from preaching something else than Christ, Paul might have so ventured to try it. He was deeply versed in all the learning of the East, a great logician, a brilliant rhetorician, having a fervid fancy, a soaring imagination, and a magnetic power over men. He might easily have brought to his feet the proud Pharisee, the stoical Scribe, the curious Greek, and the credulous Barbarian. But at his feet he knew that they would have been no better off, no nearer salvation than if they had never heard his voice. He could have interested and pleased them, but he declared, "If I yet pleased men, I should not be the servant of Christ." "I preached philosophy and men applauded; I preached Christ and men repented."

My brothers, we are not here to win men by cleverness of speech. We are to be concerned, not that men may see our handsome bow and arrows and our skillful use of the same, but that they may hear the cries of the wounded of the Lord: "Men and brethren, what must we do to be saved?" You have heard of certain preaching as an "intellectual treat," as something "perfectly grand," and all that. Our mission as preachers means nothing of the sort. If our preaching causes men to think that intellect or anything else is even to be compared with the saving of an immortal soul, then are we guilty of treason against the gospel of God's Son.

Paul had no time to deal in platitudes. To him the world was lost. On the brow of every unsaved man the awful judgment of God, "condemned already," was written in letters of Stygian blackness. This condemnation was to Paul no idle dream, but it was a present, awful reality, the contemplation of which burned in his bones like a fire and made him "count not his life dear unto himself" if only he might preach unto a lost world the "unsearchable riches of Christ."

Paul might have taken to the lecture platform to be what they now call a "moral reformer." He might have spent his days declaring against the popular sins of avarice, pride and formalism; or against the abuses and corruptions of government, and raised a world-wide riot against Roman usurpation and tyranny. He might have poured the vials of his wrath upon hypocrisy, extortion, licentiousness, and the whole category of common sins; but instead of all this, he steadfastly clung to the one sufficient theme, "Christ and Him crucified." There is now a great itch abroad in the land demanding "reform." From theology clear down to a city council, there must be an overhauling of things. The air is filled with screaming voices who propose to adjust the discordant elements of both Church and State. The rivers of reform must wash out the Augean stables everywhere, and scorching denunciation must be hurled against sin, whether in places high or low. And shall not Christ's preacher faithfully rebuke sin everywhere? Ah, yes, but His is a far larger gospel than merely that. The preaching that has Christ for its center will work every reform, and such reform will be permanent. Rightly did someone say that the proof of Christ's greatness was that He could stand before the Roman empire and never strike it. He struck deeper than external conditions—He struck the hearts of men. Though corruption reigned on every side and sin was defiant, yet He pointed men, not to outward conditions or questions, but to the eternal verities of God. The emphasis of His message was put upon God and not upon man. It was so with the Twelve; it was so with Paul; it was so with John the Baptist; it was so with God's prophets of old, it is so with every successful winner of souls.

All sins are included in the one sin of the rejection of Christ. For this reason, Paul knew—and the truth is overwhelming, eternal, divine—that though he could drive all men from their sins outwardly, yet they would still be lost eternally, without "Christ in them the hope of glory." He knew that it was worse than useless to drive all these devils out of the heart, if there was not a "strong man armed" to keep them out. Otherwise the "last state of that man would be worse than the first." He knew that if He preached Christ, the power of God unto salvation, and He was received into the heart, the expulsive power of this new affection would triumph over all sin and save the soul from death.

Fathers and brothers, in the divine vocation of the ministry, especially my young comrades in this holy warfare, let us not be triflers in our heaven-appointed mission. Contemptible is the memory of Nero—he fiddled while Rome was burning. Aeropus, of Macedonia, was one of the most insignificant kings in history, because he spent his time whittling on trifles while the supreme interests of his kingdom were disregarded. How like them both is the preacher who expends his energies upon secular and transient themes, never touching the great center of truth, and having an indifferent regard to the momentous interests of eternity. May our fidelity to Jesus be far more sublime than that of the French soldiers who so loved their Emperor that, though wounded and dying on the field of battle, with one last effort they would turn upon their elbows and cry out as he passed: "Long live the Emperor!"

O my brothers, it matters little what shall become of us if only we shall exalt the name of Christ. Our ease, our worldly prospects, our reputation, all may go for naught, if only always and everywhere we may know only this—to exalt the name of Christ.

> Happy if with my latest breath
> I may but speak His name;
> Preach Him to all, and gasp in death,
> Behold, behold, the Lamb!

But now, more briefly, let us look at the second thought deduced from the text:

II. The ministry is the heaven-appointed exponent of the mission of every redeemed soul. As Paul was saved for a specific purpose and called into a great mission, so is it true of every redeemed soul in the kingdom of God. Salvation is often too narrowly defined. It not only saves from, but also saves unto. It not only bestows unspeakable benefits, but it imposes worldwide obligations. It not only has reference to ourselves, but also we are made Christians in order that we may instrumentally make other Christians. Paul's life was one sublime effort to be true to the last command of Christ: "Go ye into all the world and preach the gospel to every creature." That command has never been revoked, nor in any wise modified, and is as binding upon us as it was upon Paul or upon those that heard it as it fell from the Master's lips on Olivet.

Christianity is essentially and fundamentally missionary. He who reads God's Word aright sees that the missionary idea is the very essence of divine revelation. It proclaims this truth with ten thousand tongues of fire. If you could but banish from the gospel the missionary idea it would never give forth another sound. No sinner would ever again be invited to Christ. No Bible would ever again be printed or circulated except as a money venture. And the whole scheme of Christianity would collapse under the superincumbent weight of an inordinate and all-prevalent selfishness.

Missions is not simply an organ of the church, but the church itself is the organ for missions. To this end the church was made—for this cause Christ brought it into the world. The work of missions therefore is not a little optional annex to a church, but it is as essential to the true work of the church as is the heart essential to the human body.

What is Christ's church? It is His body, the instrument of His purpose of which He is the head. It is the business of the head to direct and control the body. Christ, the great Head, is lawgiver and director over His body, the church. The mission of Christ's church must be identical with the mission of Christ Himself. What was His mission? Find that out and you will know the mission of every church and every individual Christian. He Himself so tells us: "As My Father hath sent Me, even so send I you." Here is the great source of the church's authority and purpose. And a church could furnish no other evidence half so strong that she is not a New Testament church as the refusal or disinclination to obey Christ's last and all-inclusive commandment. And a preacher, even though he may have been baptized and may talk much about "soundness in faith," could furnish no stronger evidence that he is not in the apostolic succession than that he is not a missionary.

High time is it that the consciences of very many people were faithfully aroused as to the nature and meaning of Christ's churches in the world. False views abound on every side. A church of Christ is not an ark in which a few of the elect are to be happily housed in order that they may float around joyfully over the drowning world beneath them. Nor is it a ship, passage upon which will land us in the heavenly country. Nor is it an insurance company, to which we may pay dues now and then, and thus certainly secure our dear selves against all loss. Nor is it a hospital for healing all manner of sickness. Nor is it a select social club with a toastmaster to call out such themes as shall provoke the building up of a mutual admiration society. Nor is it a debating society where more attention is to be given to the fine points of ecclesiasticism rather than to the consuming passion of Christianity. Nor is it a school where we may gather as students to be forever taught. Nor is it merely a place of worship where we may give ourselves to song and praise and meditation about our heavenly inheritance.

Christ's church is not any of these nor all of them combined; but with my whole heart I declare that His church exists primarily to give the gospel to all the world.

This great motive is its native air, and any church that will persistently ignore this heaven-appointed work does not have the moral right to the plat of ground on which the church building stands. Christianity is incomparably more than a creed—it is a life. Any other conception than that Christ's church is to be a soul-saving army is a caricature upon the churches of the New Testament. And the day comes on apace—may God speed its coming—when any church not missionary both in spirit and practice shall be regarded as a monstrosity, and when the regular giving of money for worldwide evangelization shall be as great a test of orthodoxy as is baptism.

Furthermore, Christ's church is to be sublimely aggressive rather than defensive. He did not mean that His soldiers should be chiefly engaged in building forts of defense. Any church that merely sits and sings "hold the fort" will soon have no fort to hold. We hear a great deal now about "expansion." I don't know what the politicians intend to make of it all, but I do know that the key-word of Christianity is expansion. "His dominion shall extend from sea to sea, and from the river unto the uttermost ends of the earth." Napoleon said, "Conquest has made me what I am and conquest must maintain me." Inviolably true is it of Christ's churches that conquest must ever be their watchword. Not only the well-being but the very being of a church depends upon its fidelity to the one design for which Christ brought it into the world. Self-preservation demands that it shall be missionary. The antimission spirit is the death of spiritual development. It is the fruitful parent of coldness, selfishness, and hardness of heart, and it is the hotbed and breeding place of suspicion, bickerings, malice, heresy and all uncharitableness. The consequences to a church without the mission spirit are so direful that it becomes a hospital, and unless it is converted, God removes its candlestick and then it becomes a graveyard. Our only safety is that we give ourselves to the supreme purpose and passion of Christianity. Yea more, our very culture shall become our hindrance if it be not inflamed and impassioned by the Spirit of Christ.

What shall be our motive for this great work? The first and supreme motive for all missionary work is the command of Jesus Christ. Surely this is an all-sufficient reason. No Christian has the right to cavil or halt one second here. Even though a thousand objections to the work might be presented, and though it were shown that it would take uncounted resources, both of men and money, to reach one single heathen, yet the duty to obey would not be altered one iota. Our Savior and King commands worldwide evangelization, and disobedience to such command for any cause is bald treachery to our trust as Christians, and cold treason against Jesus Christ.

There are many other reasons for obedience to such command, but they are unnecessary except as they may awaken our zeal and strengthen our faith. There are the motives of gratitude, and chivalry, already achieved, and still other motives, potent and urgent. But underlying all these motives and springs of action is the plain, unchangeable command of Christ.

At the bloody battle of Troy, Henry IV of France said to his soldiers: "When you lose sight of your colors, rally to my white plume. You will always find it in the way to glory." So when every other motive to missionary effort fails, this one—loyalty to Christ's command—stands firm as the adamantine hills. And loyalty to Christ, we have always made bold to say, is the fundamental principle in our denominational life. We reject utterly all assumed authority from any human source whatsoever. "One is our Master, even Christ." We boldly repudiate the right of pope or council, or anybody else, to ignore scriptural baptism, or change that ordinance in any respect from the Christ-given pattern.

O my brethren, I pause and tremble as I ask what shall be said of our loyalty to Christ's last but all-inclusive command? Take the figures: One billion human beings are without the gospel; forty million die every year; one hundred thousand die every day, four die every time we breathe; and yet, Southern Baptists are giving only a few cents a member a year for their eternal salvation! I wonder if that is the one-thousandth part of our proper loyalty to Christ on the question of money! I wonder if hundreds of men in this convention should not this hour be preaching the gospel in the regions beyond!

We shall not cease to make much of orthodoxy, but I would write it this night in letters of living fire that true orthodoxy is lacking in any preacher or church that can close the ear against the Macedonian cry of earth's perishing millions and maintain an indifferent concern to our Master's command to "go." There is a heresy of inaction as well as of precept. How much better is faith without works than works without faith? There is such a thing as a dead orthodoxy. We may orate eloquently about creeds and engage in endless discussion over the fine points of ecclesiasticism, but above all this stands out the living Word of God: "Be ye doers of the Word, and not hearers only." "If ye love Me, ye will keep My commandments." I plead for a living orthodoxy, not a dry, dead dogma, out of which has gone all the blood and heartbeat, leaving only a grinning, ghastly skeleton behind, but an orthodoxy, every pulsation of which can be felt and which is the incarnation of practical loyalty to God.

Our great people, well is it known, are sublimely set for the defense of the faith once delivered and as sublimely set against all heresy. God be thanked! May we always stand for the simple faith of the New Testament and declare that there is a difference, yea, even an impassable gulf, between truth and error. But when we do this, let us remember that the "life is more than meat and the body more than raiment." Let us remember that the deadliest of all heresies is the antimission heresy. And let us remember that the antimission heresy is the black plague of the Southern Baptist Convention.

Brethren, the hour comes to our people, and even now is, that the landmark that most of all needs resetting is the restoring of a predominant mission spirit to all our people. Let it be understood throughout all of our borders, from the blue waters of the Chesapeake to the silvery sands of the Rio Grande, that we regard as our life business the evangelization of the world; that all our denominational enterprises have utterly missed their purpose, if they do not stand for the central truth of Christianity. Let this be true of our denominational papers, of our Christian colleges, of yonder matchless Theological Seminary. Oh, when we have as much Christianity as we have orthodoxy, then will we soon take the world for Jesus!

It is said that over the door of the Alhambra, an old Moorish palace, on the one side, carved in stone, was a book, and on the other side, reaching out to clasp the book, was a hand. In connection with this there was a legend that someday the hand would clasp the book and then the Alhambra would fall. That old Moorish palace may be taken as a symbol of the dark kingdom of evil in the earth—Satan's Alhambra, for whose subjugation and destruction God's people go forth to war. When will Satan's stronghold be beaten down and the victory of God's people be complete? It will be when the hand clasps the Book. The hand is the hand of Duty and the Book is the book of Doctrine, and when duty and doctrine go forth united in the fullness and power of meaning intended of God, then shall the Alhambra of sin speedily totter to its everlasting doom and Christ shall be exalted Lord over all forevermore!

Brethren, I believe that the hour of destiny has come to our people. The voice of God's providence rings out louder than the voice of many waters, "Go forward!" Every Red Sea of difficulty has been divided and the gates to all the nations stand ajar. A little while ago the obstacles everywhere seemed insuperable. An impassable wall surrounded China. The ports of Japan were entirely sealed. The Dark Continent was impenetrable, even to the explorer. The isles of the ocean were thronged with cannibals more to be dreaded than all the dangers of the sea. Now the doors swing wide open to every people. Japan is white to the harvest. India is restless to hear of Jesus. The great men of China yearn to know the oracles of God. Mohammed's crescent wanes and the shrines of every false religion now are tottering and their idols begin to crumble into dust. The nations are impressible as the wax. The signs of the times, the policies of governments, the majestic march of events, are all instinct with divine meanings and are the true burning bush whereby God is mightily revealing Himself to the world. At last, even the very elements of nature have all been laid under tribute for the forwarding of the chariot. We stand facing the opportunity of the ages. My brothers, in the presence of such matchless opportunities, in this day of the right hand of God, ought not every man of us to cease from all minor things and join in the sublime effort at once to give the gospel to the world?

A French drummer boy was once urged by a fleeing officer to "beat a retreat," and the boy replied, "Sire, I cannot beat a retreat, but oh, I can beat a forward march that would make the dead fall into line." O Baptists of the South, let us from this Convention beat a forward march, the spirit of which shall penetrate our churches like a flame of fire, and this year call forth men and money in such wondrous fashion as shall fill the whole earth with astonishment and demonstrate that our only concern this side of heaven is to be loyal to Jesus Christ. Brethren, I believe that even Satan himself marvels at our slowness. Israel took forty years to make a journey that ought to have been made in a few days. We are doing that very thing today. One thousand of our churches in the South ought to support one missionary each for the coming year. God give us obedience to such heavenly vision!

For a long, long while there came on every sighing breezing from the fair isle of Cuba a piteous cry for help. At last our land rose up and with men and money went forth and gave relief. Adown the centuries there has come an unceasing cry in tones of tenderest love: "I thirst." I hear it even now, "I thirst." Whose is the voice? It is the voice of Jesus dying on the cross, "I thirst." That thirst has never yet been quenched. He thirsts for China, for Asia and Africa, for the Filipinos, for poor lost men wherever found. O let us rise up and quench His thirst! Then shall He see the travail of His soul and be satisfied. And all the redeemed shall be satisfied with Him, and from all their blood-washed lips this glad hosanna shall ring out forever: Emmanuel—God with us!